This is the German Shorthaired and Wirehaired
Pointer

THIS IS THE GERMAN SHORTHAIRED AND WIREHAIRED POINTER

by Louise Ziegler Spirer
and
Herbert F. Spirer

Distributed in the U.S.A. by T.F.H. Publications, Inc., 211 West Sylvania Avenue, P.O. Box 27, Neptune City, N.J. 07753; in England by T.F.H. (Gt. Britain) Ltd., 13 Nutley Lane, Reigate, Surrey; in Canada to the book store and library trade by Clarke, Irwin & Company, Clarwin House, 791 St. Clair Avenue West, Toronto 10, Ontario; in Canada to the pet trade by Rolf C. Hagen Ltd., 3225 Sartelon Street, Montreal 382, Quebec; in Southeast Asia by Y.W. Ong, 9 Lorong 36 Geylang, Singapore 14; in Australia and the south Pacific by Pet Imports Pty. Ltd., P.O. Box 149, Brookvale 2100, N.S.W., Australia. Published by T.F.H. Publications Inc. Ltd., The British Crown Colony of Hong Kong.

Frontispiece: The German Pointers were bred as dual purpose hunters at a time when big game was plentiful in Germany and on the Continent. When the larger game animals became scarce the two breeds were turned to bird work at which both excel.

Photo Credits

Ann Krausse, Percy T. Jones, Stephen Klein, C. M. Cooke & Son, Bill Francis, Bennett Associates, William Brown, William Gilbert, Joan Ludwig, Frasie Studio, Cliff Oliver, Evelyn Shafer, Louise Van der Meid

ISBN 0-87666-303-X

Contents

ACKNOWLEDGMENTS

For the cooperation and encouragement of Mr. and Mrs. Arthur W. Viner of Stamford, Conn., and their fine Shorthairs, Cassandra of Hollabird and Franz of Hunting Ridge, the authors are most grateful. The editorial assistance of Mr. and Mrs. Matthew Kenny was invaluable in helping to see this book to completion.

German Pointers have not achieved a place of prominence among purebred dogs without good reason. These highly intelligent dogs have proven themselves equal to almost any role a dog could be asked to fill in competition, sport or family life.

Introduction

At last you have the dog of your dreams. Today is the day you bring home your purebred German Shorthaired or Wirehaired Pointer. Perhaps you are already thinking of the pleasures of hunting with one of the most versatile hunters in dogdom or anticipating the fun and companionship of this all-round dog.

You have consulted the experts, visited the dog shows and local gun clubs, examined many litters of German Pointers, and finally found the puppy *you* want. And here he is—home with you. He's probably scared and lonely for his mother, brothers and sisters, uncertain about his new master, and hungry and tired. You too may be uncertain. You are now responsible for this small bundle of energy—responsible for his care, housing, training, grooming, feeding and health. You are responsible both to your family and your neighbors for a well-trained, healthy, and happy dog.

Welcome your dog, show him his bed, offer him a little warm milk or formula (if you received some from the kennel or owners) and cuddle him a little. Soon you will be good friends and sure of each other.

Your dog's breeder has spent many hours studying German Shorthaired and Wirehaired Pointers and scientifically breeding them to obtain the best possible dogs. He has been careful with the diet and kennel care of his dogs. But no amount of scientific breeding and no amount of early care can make up for what *you* must do to rear a healthy dog. This book is intended to offer helps and hints for the care of your dog, and we suggest you read it through carefully. It will guide you through the many phases of dog life. This is a practical book for you, the dog-owner; it makes no claim to offer instant cures and sure-fire solutions to your every problem. It is no substitute for the licensed veterinarian when your dog is ill.

In the meantime, enjoy your dog. He is one of the most adaptable of all dogs. Equally at home in the field or kennel, he is protective of his family, gentle with children, an excellent companion and guardian of hearth and home. Kindly treated and well cared for, he will always be a pleasure.

Chapter I

History

Man's best friend since the dawn of history, the dog has served him as guardian, herder and provider. The dog's intelligence and steadfast loyalty have always set him apart from other domesticated animals. In return for this faithful service, man has fed and housed his pet— and celebrated him in song, story, painting and sculpture.

ANCIENT HISTORY

The ancient dog and wolf were closely related, with common ancestors and similar behavior. Prehistoric dogs hunted in packs, as wolves still do, and used their cunning and physical strength to run down game. By the time dog joined man, there were several distinct types of dogs similar to the Mastiff, Hound or Shepherd. The wolf was left behind to develop his own family history—his cousins include the jackal, coyote, dingo and fox, all of whom resemble the dog.

Archaeologists believe that ancient man distinguished between the character and abilities of the different types of dogs—the Shepherd was used to guard flocks of sheep and goats, the Hound hunted with his master, and (later) the Mastiff accompanied soldiers in battle. As man changed from nomad to farmer, he trained the herding dogs to guard his hearth as well as his flocks.

The cave paintings found in southern France are the oldest known paintings, believed to be more than 50,000 years old. The unknown artists who painted these pictures included scenes which show dogs similar to Shepherds or Alsatians, hunting with man in his constant search for food.

Archaeologists have also found dog remains in Neolithic family sites in England, and in a 5,000 year-old-Chinese village the bones of dogs were found mixed in with those of sheep and pigs.

Many dogs are also shown in the paintings and picture-like hieroglyphics of the ancient Egyptians, who left almost complete records

Ch. Adam's Rib of Rocky Run, owned and handled by Robert H. McKowen. Sire: Ch. Adam V. Fuehrerheim; dam: Ch. Rocky Run's Poldi. Bred by Robert L. Arnold, Rib is shown finishing his championship at the Lancaster Kennel Club under judge John Ward Brady. This fine Shorthair finished in four shows and won five derby classes at field trials.

of their lives in the tombs of their Pharaohs. Dogs are clearly shown as sheepherders and hunters. The Pharaohs are pictured hunting with packs of Hounds, easily identified as Basset, Mastiff or Terrier-like dogs.

The Greeks and Romans kept dogs as house pets as well as for their usefulness. One of the Greek dogs was placed in the heavens—Sirius, the Dog Star, follows his master, Orion the Hunter, across the skies. The Romans, with their talent for organization, had apparently distinguished six distinct classes of dogs: Shepherds like the Husky and Chow; Scent Hounds (the Romans hunted with Bloodhounds); Greyhounds like the Saluki and Afghan; sporting types similar to the Setter, Retriever and Poodle; and military dogs such as the Bulldog, Great Dane and Boxer.

Many of the famed Roman mosaics depict dogs. A common type was a large mosaic before the household door, showing a vigilant watchdog and carrying the inscription *cave canem* (beware the dog). The Romans also kept dogs as pets, and small wooden and ceramic dogs have been found among their children's toys.

Ch. Brownridge Marga, owned by Mrs. M. Layton.

Man developed dogs for the chase before he molded the canine tribe into other forms. Modern bird dogs came about when hunting became a sport rather than a necessity of life.

EARLY HISTORY OF HUNTING DOGS

In prehistoric times, both man and dog depended on hunting to supply their food, and in this common activity man and dog joined forces as they do today. As man turned to farming for his food supply, hunting became sport rather than necessity, and the common man found that his hunting was often outlawed as vast game preserves, the playgrounds of kings and nobility, spread across Europe. The peasants, serfs, and villeins did little hunting other than poaching on the forbidden preserves, but the nobility hunted with packs of dogs and large retinues of men. Many hunts were great social occasions, and we have many early descriptions of these occasions in song and story. Chaucer and Francois Villon told of the dog, and Gaston Phoebus, Comte de Foix (1631-1691), who kept sixteen hundred dogs, wrote one of the earliest accounts of hunting, called *The Master of Game.*

Because of the great interest in hunting, the nobility kept great packs of hunting dogs and encouraged breeding and training dogs for just this purpose. In the Middle Ages, hunting was brought to a state of perfection. When members of royalty hunted, they rode with their dogs and many trainers and keepers. Nets were used before the invention of the rifle. These were spread over large areas where small game was known to be located (areas were often "seeded" especially for the hunters), and the dogs used to flush the game into the nets. Falcons, which not only found but also killed and retrieved game,

Ch. Springfarm Sandpiper, owned by Mrs. D. Johnson.

were used for feathered and furred game, but falconry did not require dogs.

Hawking, however, was also a popular sport, and these birds of prey were usually accompanied by Greyhounds and Pointers. Hawks were used to hunt such low-lying game as ducks and rabbits.

Medieval painters often showed the lord of the manor with his dog or hunters. Frans Snyders (1579-1657) shows packs of dogs accompanying hunters, and Pisanello (1397-1455) in his famous painting *The Vision of St. Eustace* pictures several hunting dogs, one of them avidly pursuing a rabbit. One of the earliest examples of the German Pointer can be seen in a fine woodcut of a falconer's room, carved by Jost Ammons (1534-1590), who also portrayed dogs in other pictures.

The role of the hunting dog became more important when the rifle was invented. Dogs were used to point (locate) the game and flush it, and the hunter found it an easy matter to bring down the

Sh. Ch. Appleine Chough, owned by Mrs. C. Appleton.

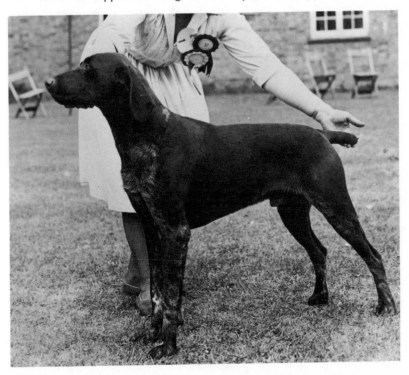

game with the far-reaching rifle. Hunters no longer required horses to pursue game; a hike in the fields with dogs and gun was sufficient.

Hunting was introduced into Germany after the Thirty Years War. The Germans imported French Pointers to whom they spoke in French, and Hounds which were instructed in German. In the wave of enthusiasm for hunting, dogs were also imported from Spain and Italy. It is significant to note that in 1677 the Count of Darmstadt kept 10 Pointers, and by 1770 every forester had at least two Pointers. Germany has since played a key role in the development of all-purpose hunting dogs such as the German Shorthaired Pointer.

HISTORY OF THE GERMAN SHORTHAIRED POINTER

Germany: Among the Pointers imported into Germany during this rapid growth of hunting in the 17th century was the Old Spanish Pointer. This dog was an excellent pointer of game, but the German

All of the Pointer breeds come from the same root stock. They not only share basic physical similarity, but they all have in common the instinctive desire to hunt.

Ch. Gretchenhof Cimarron, bred by Gretchenhof Kennels. This group-winning bitch is shown in a good breed win being handled by Walter Shallenbarger.

hunter wanted greater scenting ability and crossed the Spanish Pointer with the Bloodhound. The resulting dog was a fine, big, houndy dog with an excellent nose and improved trailing and pointing abilities. He had a waterproof coat and webbed feet and could be used for water as well as land retrieving. Known as the Old German Pointer, he served the hunter satisfactorily for many years, despite his somewhat heavy build and slow motion.

By the latter part of the 19th century, hunting in Germany was widespread, a favorite pastime of the common man as well as the nobility. As the number of hunters multiplied, however, the available hunting areas shrank because of cultivation, industrialization, and the increasing population.

For hunting in these restricted areas, a good all-around hunter was required. A dog which could work light as well as heavy cover on land

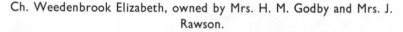

Ch. Weedenbrook Elizabeth, owned by Mrs. H. M. Godby and Mrs. J. Rawson.

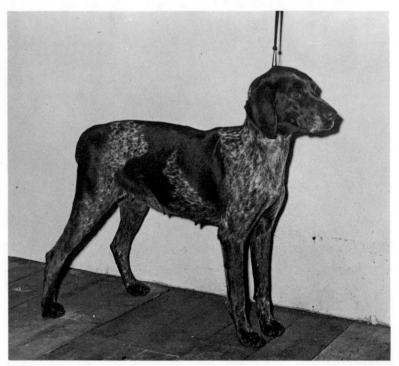

and also in water was called for, and the German breeders met this requirement with great success. Knowing their exact goals, they crossed many of their hunting breeds to achieve them. And the German Shorthaired Pointer is surely a triumph of crossbreeding.

About 1870, the Old German Pointer developed from the Old Spanish Pointer and Bloodhound cross was crossed with the English Pointer. The English Pointer itself is a mixture of Old Spanish Pointer and English Foxhound, as well as other related breeds. An example of the specialized type of dog preferred by the English, the English Pointer was light, fast and far-ranging. This generally accepted origin of the German Shorthaired Pointer is illustrated graphically in the table below:

$$
\left.
\begin{array}{l}
\left. \begin{array}{l} \text{Old Spanish Pointer} \\ \quad\times \\ \text{Bloodhound} \end{array} \right\} = \text{Old German Pointer} \\
\qquad\qquad\qquad\qquad\qquad \times \\
\left. \begin{array}{l} \text{Old Spanish Pointer} \\ \quad\times \\ \text{English Foxhound} \end{array} \right\} = \text{English Pointer}
\end{array}
\right\} = \text{German Shorthaired Pointer}
$$

Thus the German Shorthaired Pointer met the German hunter's requirements for a single "universal" hunting dog, one which could scent, point, and retrieve most feathered and furred game, and even trail large wounded animals, at home on land or water.

As we could expect, the dog rapidly became popular in Germany. The first registration in the German Kennel Stud Book was in 1872; the first official pedigree was issued in 1899. There were many fine kennels which established the foundation stock of the German Short-haired Pointer, among them the kennels of Herr L. Schmidt and those of V. Moabit and V. Stolpshof. Hektor I and Treff 1010 are believed to be among the "founding fathers" of the breed, and Mars Altenau 69P and Artus Sand 1830V are also considered pillars of the German Shorthaired Pointer stock. In the next 25 years, the type was set.

Other Countries: The Italians called the breed the *Braque Allemand* and have bred many. The breed has become known wherever hunting is a popular sport, particularly in continental Europe and the United States. The English preference for specialized dogs, Pointers, Retrievers and Terriers, has limited their use in English hunting, although many more Shorthairs may find their way into English households as the sport spreads.

THE GERMAN SHORTHAIRED POINTER IN AMERICA

We do not know exactly when the first German Shorthaired Pointer crossed the Atlantic, but some of them must have traveled here with the waves of German immigration in the late 19th century. Many must have settled in the Midwest, where they are still very popular. One picture of a German Shorthaired Pointer was found in the old family album of one of these early German immigrants. The dog's name, appropriately, was "Sport". The first official German Shorthaired Pointer to arrive was imported around 1925 by Dr. Charles Thornton of Montana, who set up a kennel to breed Shorthairs. The breed was recognized in 1930 by the AKC, and Grief v d Flei-

The German Shorthaired Pointer has made many friends wherever people who appreciate good dogs are to be found. In America he is one of the most highly respected of Sporting dogs and probably the most popular of the Continental Pointers.

Ch. Ferrier Jaeger, owned by Mr. M. Meredith-Hardy.

gerhalde was the first dog enrolled. The growth of popularity has been slow. In 1947 there were only 4,628 Shorthairs registered, but this figure increased shortly thereafter, and by 1955 there were over 15,000 registered with the AKC. They are now among the fifty most popular breeds, and there are increasing numbers enrolled in the Field Dog Stud Book, which registers sporting breeds.

The emphasis in this country has been on the lighter, faster dog, and there has been much effort by breeders to improve the stock. Jack Shattuck, who owned the Schwabenberg Kennels, is known as an outstanding breeder, and Rusty v Schwabenberg was the first dual champ in the AKC registry. He was also a winners' dog twice at Westminster and has been bred extensively. Maida v Thalbeck, bred by Joseph Burkhart, produced four champions, proving that it runs in the family! A truly outstanding effort was made by dam Jane v Grunen Adler II when she produced 11 pups in one litter. They were named after important people then in the news, such as Franklin D. Roosevelt, Herbert Hoover and John L. Lewis.

As a current indication of the popularity of this hunting dog, you have only to read over issues of the *German Shorthaired Pointer News* to see the mushrooming of clubs, both specialty and gun clubs, and the number of Shorthairs run in field trials.

CHARACTERISTICS WHICH HISTORY BRED

Today's specialized breeds of dogs are the results of controlled breedings; they didn't spring up by accident. Dog owners and breeders wanted certain types of dogs for specific purposes and, because of this desire, encouraged purebreds. In the case of the Shorthair, the breeders make no secret of the number of crossbred dogs

Sh. Ch. Sparrowswick Weiss Jäger, owned by Mrs. J. Plumtree.

Ch. Lucky of Pheasant Hill, owned by William J. Stoppelbein and bred by Eugene L. Keeth. Sire F. T. Ch. Zitt V.D. Sellweide; dam: Ursel V. Assegrunde. This useful-looking bitch is shown in a win under the late Mrs. Alfred LePine, handler, Durwood L. Van Zandt.

bred into the line. This crossbreeding was done with care, as the breeders encouraged characteristics they wanted and bred out undesirable qualities.

The early German Pointers were fine for pointing, but they needed better noses. Early breeders, noting the excellent nose of the Bloodhound, crossed the Pointer with this breed. Later, when hunters demanded a lighter, faster, all-around dog, they crossbred with the English Pointer. Breeders bred in an oily, dense undercoat in order to keep the coat short and waterproof. As the cover became lighter and more dogs hunted in the open rather than in dense forests, liver and white ticked Pointers were encouraged, as they stood out in the fields of weed and stubble. The German sportsman insists that the Shorthair hunt a "mixed bag" and expects him to be equally at home on land or water. In America, the Shorthair is not used as extensively as on the Continent. He is not expected to hunt large game animals, and he is used more for feathered game such as pheasants, woodcock and quail, and bred for speed, lightness and wide range. There are some dog historians who believe that English Pointer blood was infused here rather than in Germany, for this purpose.

THE GERMAN WIREHAIRED POINTER

The German Wirehaired Pointer is a new dog to many Americans and is often confused with the Wirehaired Pointing Griffon. The Germans bred a number of different types of Pointers; the Wirehaired Pointer (or Drahthaar) is just one of several. At present, however, there are more Wirehaired Pointers registered in Germany than Shorthairs. The Wirehair appears to be a cross between the Pointer, the Foxhound and the Poodle. There is speculation that Terrier blood is also mixed in, accounting for the breed's similarity to the Airedale or Schnauzer. Some people also speculate that both the Shorthair and the Wirehair came from common stock.

The earliest Wirehaired Pointer Club in Germany was the Deutsch-Drahthaar, which had four main types of dogs enrolled— the Deutsch-Drahthaar; the Pudelpointer, a combination of Poodle and English Pointer; the Stickelhaar; and the Griffon, both of which have mixed Pointer, Foxhound, Pudelpointer and Polish Water Dog blood. It is possible that there was some interbreeding among all these breeds from which the modern-day German Wirehaired Pointer emerged.

The German Wirehaired Pointer was produced to serve the German sportsman who demanded a tough, capable partner in the field that would act as an all-around hunter. He was recognized by the American Kennel Club in 1959 and has made a steady increase in popularity among pet owners and hunters ever since.

In Germany today the German Wirehair outranks his Shorthaired counterpart in number of registrations. The reverse is true in the United States, but it must be borne in mind that the requirements of the American hunter are different, and the Wirehair is a comparative newcomer in the United States.

The Wirehair was first recognized in Germany in 1870 and has increased in popularity there. It was imported into the United States in 1920 but not officially recognized until 1959. The first dog to win an AKC field championship was Herr Baron's Mike, in 1959. Mr. and Mrs. A. H. Gallagher, Wirehaired Pointer enthusiasts, are credited with acquainting the American hunter with this dog, and Mr. Gallagher also founded the German Wirehaired Pointer Club of America. The Wirehair has since become a favorite with many sportsmen.

Chapter II

Description

When you first went dog-hunting, did you know that you wanted a German Shorthaired Pointer or Wirehaired Pointer?

Many people see a dog in a store window, and he is such a cute puppy that they immediately dash off and buy one just like him, or even buy that "doggie in the window".

Others come to like a dog they see in someone's house and ask where they can purchase a similar one. Or if one of the dogs in the neighborhood has a litter of puppies, you will often see some of her children in nearby homes (though some people prefer to send their look-alikes to other areas).

Still others, scientific in their selection of a dog, go to the library and look up different breeds of dogs, or write to the American Kennel Club for advice and information. Or they may find their dogs through the dog magazines which advertise puppies for sale.

For the serious hunter, the many fine qualities of the German Shorthaired or Wirehaired Pointer in the field, plus his versatility, may be the chief reason for the choice.

While you may have obtained your dog through any of the channels mentioned above, your Shorthair is not a common dog. Although he is increasing in popularity, he is still not found in as many homes as, for example, the Poodle, and he has many rivals in the field. But he does have some very special qualities and you will want to know what your Shorthair is like, temperamentally and physically.

GERMAN SHORTHAIRED POINTER

The German Shorthaired Pointer is a dog of middle size, powerful and muscular. He needs adequate space to keep him in tone and lots of protein to maintain his powerful, energetic body. He is an excellent housedog, loyal and protective.

This Pointer is noted for his versatile hunting ability. He was bred for both pointing and retrieving. His short, water-repellent coat serves both in heavy land cover and in water. The German Short-haired Pointer is ideal for the one-dog hunter who cannot afford or does not wish a kennel-full of dogs. He has a fine nose and instinctive pointing and retrieving ability, and his powerful build allows him to range far and spend long hours in the field. Because of this all-around utility, breeders have encouraged these characteristics in the breed.

AKC STANDARDS

The American Kennel Club sets the standards for all breeds of pedigreed dogs in America. No dog can be the complete ideal, but show winners are generally those dogs which come closest to the ideal. If you are buying a dog for show purposes, it is wise to check the points you need, as well as the dog's ancestors. Even if you just want

Ch. Ludwig Von Osthoff, owned and bred by Charles and Florence Weckerle was a prominent winner in the Midwest during the early sixties. He is shown here taking best in show at the Winnegamie Kennel Club under the late Mrs. Alfred LePine, handler Hollis Wilson.

Ch. Gretchenhof White Frost, owned by Margo Bryant and bred by Gretchenhof Kennels. This fine best in show winner is seen here with handler Erik Thomee.

a dog for the home, you may still want to purchase a dog which conforms closely to the standard, for some day you may wish to have a litter, and the best bred dogs are the most in demand as dams and sires. Selecting a dog carefully also discourages those few unscrupulous breeders who turn out dogs with little regard for the quality of the breed.

A *fault* is a departure from the ideal. It is not enough to disqualify a dog from the show ring, but it hurts his chances of winning.

A *disqualifying fault* disqualifies a dog from showing. It is of a more serious nature than a fault.

STANDARD FOR THE GERMAN SHORTHAIRED POINTER

The standard by which the German Shorthaired Pointer is judged is drawn up by the German Shorthaired Pointer Club of America, Inc., and approved by the Board of Directors of the American Kennel Club.

General Appearance: The over-all picture which is created in the observer's eye should be that of an aristocratic, well-balanced, symmetrical animal with conformation indicating power, endurance, agility and a look of intelligence and animation.

The dog should be neither unduly small nor conspicuously large. It should rather give the impression of medium size, but be like the proper hunter, with a "short back but standing over plenty of ground". Tall, leggy individuals seldom possess endurance or sound movement.

Dogs which are ponderous or unbalanced because of excess substance should be definitely rejected. The first impression should be that of a keenness which denotes full enthusiasm for work without indication of nervous or flighty character. Movement should be alertly co-ordinated without waste motion.

The good Shorthair should have grace of outline, clean-cut head, sloping shoulders, deep breast, powerful back, strong quarters, good bone composition, adequate muscle, well-carried tail, and taut coat, all of which should combine to produce a look of nobility and an indication of anatomical structure essential to correct gait which must indicate a heritage of purposefully conducted breeding.

Head: Clean-cut, neither too light nor too heavy, in proper proportion to the body. Skull should be reasonably broad, arched on side and slightly round on top. Scissura (median line between the eyes at the forehead) not too deep, occipital bone not as conspicuous as in the case of the Pointer.

The foreface should rise gradually from nose to forehead, not resembling the Roman nose. This is more strongly pronounced in the male than in the bitch, as befitting his sex. The chops should fall away from the somewhat projecting nose. Lips should be full and deep, never flewed. The chops should not fall over too much, but form a proper fold in the angle. The jaw should be powerful and the muscles well developed.

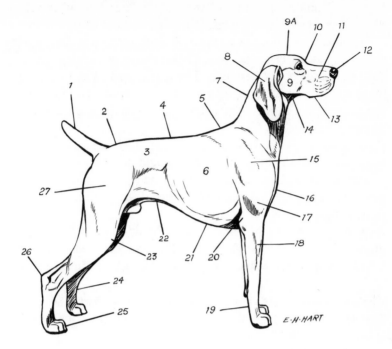

E·H·HART

Parts of the German Pointer (Shorthair Model)

1. Tail or Stern	14. Throat
2. Croup	15. Shoulder (Scapula)
3. Loin	16. Forechest
4. Back	17. Humerus (Upper Arm)
5. Withers	18. Foreleg
6. Ribs	19. Pastern
7. Neck	20. Elbow
8. Ear Leather	21. Brisket
9. Cheek	22. Tuck-Up
9A. Skull	23. Point of Stifle
10. Stop	24. Metatarsus
11. Muzzle	25. Rear feet
12. Nose	26. Hock Joint
13. Lip or Flew	27. Thigh

The line to the forehead should rise gradually and should never possess a definite stop as in the case of the Pointer, but rather a stop-effect when viewed from the side, due to the position of the eyebrows.

The muzzle should be sufficiently long to enable the dog to seize properly and to facilitate his carrying game for a long time. A pointed muzzle is not desirable. The entire head should never give the impression of tapering to a point. The depth should be in the right proportion to the length, both in the muzzle and in the skull proper.

Ears: Ears should be broad and set fairly high, lie flat, and never hang away from the head. Placement should be above eye level.

The ears, when laid in front without being pulled, should about meet the lip angle. In the case of heavier dogs, they should be correspondingly longer.

Assembly of Front Members: The shoulders should be sloping, movable, well covered with muscle. The shoulder blades should lie flat. The upper arm (also called the cross bar, i.e., the bones between

The German Shorthair's head should always look the part of an essential tool in the hunt. The head and expression should give the combined expression of strength and friendliness.

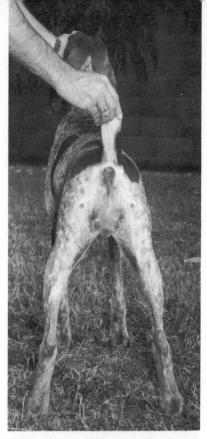

When viewing the animal's front there should be obvious power without excessive lumber. The elbows should turn neither in nor out.

A strong rear will allow the dog to work all day without tiring. When viewed from behind the hocks should not turn and the legs should appear straight.

the shoulder and elbow joints) should be as long as possible, standing away somewhat from the trunk so that the straight and closely muscled legs, when viewed from in front, should appear to be parallel. Elbows which stand away from the body or are pressed right into same indicate toes turning inwards or outwards, which should be regarded as faults. Pasterns should be strong, short, and nearly vertical.

Feet: Should be compact, close-knit and round to spoon-shaped, with the toes sufficiently arched and heavily nailed. The pad should be strong and hard.

Coat and Skin: The skin should look close and tight.

The hair should be short and thick and feel tough and hard; it is somewhat longer on the underside of the tail and the back edge of the haunches. It is softer, thinner, and shorter on the ears and the head.

Tail: Is set high and firm and must be docked, leaving approximately two-fifths of its original length.

The tail hangs down when the dog is quiet, is held horizontally when he is walking, never turned over the back or considerably bent, but violently wagged when he is on the search.

Bones: Thin and fine bones are by no means desirable in a dog which should be able to work over any and every country and should possess strength. The main importance accordingly is laid not so much on the size of the bones as on bone size in proper proportion to the body. Dogs with coarse bones are handicapped in agility of movement and speed.

Ch. Jason of Caesaromagnus, owned by Mr. and Mrs J. N. Thackery.

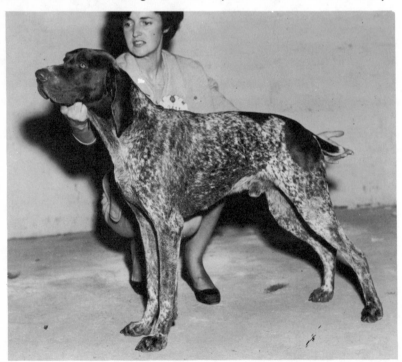

Badly cow hocked

A Good Rear

Dewclaws on rear legs. An especially
bad fault for sporting dogs

Out at elbow,
Too broad,
Loaded shoulders,
Toeing In

A good front

Shallow, narrow front,
East to west, Thin feet

 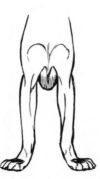 

Soft back, Short, low-set ears, Muzzle too short and square, Wet throat, Short, heavy neck, Shoulders too far forward, Over-angulated behind. Soft pasterns.

Light eye, Over-long ears, Lacks stop, Weak muzzle, Tendency to Roman nose, Shoulder assembly set too far forward, Shelly, Roach back, Over-long tail, Lack of hind angulation, Too long in loin.

A Standard of a breed is based on the work that breed was meant to perform. The Standards of both German Pointers describe the most useful dog afield and the best of both breeds emulate these utilitarian hunting qualities.

Desirable Weight and Height: Dogs—55 to 70 pounds. Bitches —45 to 60 pounds.

Dogs—23 to 25 inches. Bitches—21 to 23 inches at the shoulders.
Color: Solid liver, liver and white spotted, liver and white spotted and ticked, liver and white ticked, liver roan. Any colors other than liver and white (gray white) are not permitted.

Symmetry and field quality are most essential.

A dog well balanced in all points is preferable to one with outstanding good qualities and defects. A smooth, lithe gait is most desirable.
Faults: Bone structure too clumsy or too light, head too large, too many wrinkles in forehead, dish-faced, snipey muzzle, ears too long, pointy or fleshy, flesh-colored nose, eyes too light, too round or too closely set together, excessive throatiness, cowhocks, feet or elbows turned inward or outward, down on pasterns, loose shoulders, sway-back; black coat or tri-colored, any colors except liver or some combination of liver and white.

Dual Ch. Haar Baron's Hans, owned by Genevieve Capstaff. This typical specimen has achieved success both in field and on bench, the true measure of a useful sporting dog.

GERMAN WIREHAIRED POINTER

The German Wirehaired Pointer is a new dog on the American hunting scene. He closely resembles the German Shorthaired Pointer. His build is less sturdy but rather slender and agile. Like other wirehaired breeds, he has heavy eyebrows, whiskers, and beard, giving him a lively, happy expression.

AKC STANDARDS

The German Wirehaired Pointer is a dog that is essentially Pointer in type, of sturdy build, lively manner, and an intelligent, determined expression. In disposition the dog has been described as energetic, rather aloof but not unfriendly.

Head: The head is moderately long, the skull broad, the occipital bone not too prominent. The stop is medium, the muzzle fairly long with nasal bone straight and broad, the lips a trifle pendulous, but close and bearded. The nose is dark brown, with nostrils wide open, and the teeth are strong, with scissors bite. The ears are rounded but not too broad, and close to the sides of the head. Eyes are brown, medium in size, oval in contour, bright and clear and overhung with bushy eyebrows. Yellow eyes are not desirable. The neck is of medium length, slightly arched and devoid of dewlap; in fact, the skin throughout is notably tight to the body.

Body and Tail: The body is a little longer than it is high, (ratio 10 to 9) with the back short, straight, and strong. The entire back line should show a perceptible slope down from the withers to croup. The chest is deep and capacious, the ribs well sprung, loins taut and slender, the tuck-up apparent. Hips are broad, with croup nicely rounded and the tail docked approximately two-fifths of original length.

Legs and Feet: Forelegs are straight, with shoulders obliquely set and elbows close. The thighs are strong and muscular. The hind legs are moderately angulated at stifle and hock and, as viewed from behind, parallel to each other. Round in outline, the feet are webbed,

Ch. Oldmill Flint, owned by Dr. U. D. Mostosky and bred by N. L. Compere. Sire: Ch. Oldmill Casanova; dam: Heidi of Oldmill. A winner and sire of winners, he looks the part of a dog that can do, with ease, the work that the breed was developed for.

arched high with toes close, their pads thick and hard, and their nails strong and quite heavy. Leg bones are flat rather than round, and strong, but not so heavy or coarse as to militate against the dog's natural agility.

Coat: The coat is weather resisting and to some extent water repellent. The undercoat dense enough in winter to insulate against the cold but so thin in summer as to be almost invisible. The distinctive outer coat is straight, harsh, wiry, and rather flat-lying, from $1\frac{1}{2}$ to 2 inches in length; it is long enough to protect against the punishment of rough cover but not so long as to hide the outline. On the lower legs it is shorter and closer fitting, while over the shoulders and around the tail it is very dense and heavy. The tail is nicely coated, particularly on the underside, but devoid of feather. These dogs have bushy eyebrows of strong, straight hair and beards and whiskers of medium length.

A short, smooth coat, a soft woolly coat, or an excessively long coat is to be severely penalized.

Color: The coat is liver and white, usually either liver and white spotted, liver roan, liver and white spotted with ticking and roaning or sometimes solid liver. The nose is dark brown, sometimes with a white blaze, the ears brown. Any black in the coat is to be severely penalized. Spotted and flesh-colored noses are undesirable and are to be penalized.

Size: Height of males should be from 24-26 inches at the withers; bitches smaller, but not under 22 inches.

Eyes: The eyes should be of medium size, full of intelligence and expressive, good-humored, and yet radiating energy, neither protruding nor sunk. The eyelids should close well.

The best color is a dark shade of brown. Light yellow, china or wall eyes (bird of prey) are not desirable.

Teeth: The teeth should be strong and healthy. The molars should intermesh properly. Incisors should fit close in a true scissors bite. Jaws should be neither overshot nor undershot.

Neck: Of adequate length to permit the jaws reaching game to be retrieved, sloping downward on beautifully curving lines. The nape should be rather muscular, becoming gradually larger towards the shoulders. Moderate houndlike throatiness permitted.

Breast and Thorax: The breast in general should give the impression of depth rather than breadth; for all that, it should be in correct proportion to the other parts of the body with fair depth of chest.

The ribs forming the thorax should be well curved and not flat; they should not be absolutely round or barrel-shaped. Ribs that are entirely round prevent the necessary expansion of the chest when taking breath. The back ribs should reach well down.

The circumference of the breast immediately behind the elbows should be smaller than that of the breast about a hand's-breadth behind elbows, so that the upper arm has room for movement.

Back and Loins: Back should be short, strong, and straight, with slight rise from root of tail to withers. Excessively long or hog-backed should be penalized. Loins strong, of moderate length and slightly arched. Tuck-up should be apparent.

Assembly of Back Members: The hips should be broad with hip sockets wide apart and falling slightly toward the tail in a graceful curve. Thighs strong and well muscled. Stifles well bent. Hock joints should be well angulated, with strong straight bone structure from hock to pad. Angulation of both stifle and hock joints should be such as to combine maximum of both drive and traction. Hocks should turn neither in nor out.

SHOWING YOUR DOG

Are you tempted to show your dog? If you are, be prepared, for with all its pleasures and rewards, it is a trial of both dog and master.

Many areas have dog shows for pet owners. Your child can take his pet to the neighborhood pet show, and he will be just as proud of his dog's ribbon as if it had come from the Westminster Dog Show itself! We can remember the commotion in our house when our first dog, of somewhat mixed parentage, was made ready for her debut in the school pet show. How she was washed, combed, and brushed. Ginnie just bloomed under all the special attention and she even won a ribbon—for the best behaved dog in the show! Most children enjoy seeing their dogs entered in a show, and it is good training for both pet and master.

But a *bona fide* dog show is another thing again. There are three types of shows—the bench show and the field and obedience trials. Field trials are discussed in Chapter IX, Training. In these shows, dogs are judged on their utility—hunting, retrieving, pulling a sled, etc. Obeying commands and broadjumping are just some of the tests.

It is at the bench shows that you see your best-bred dogs vying for the best-in-show award. These dogs represent the ideal in dogdom —well bred, handsomely groomed, and beautifully behaved. The term *bench show* arises because the dogs are assigned to benches, where they remain until they are led into the show ring.

The first show held in America was in Chicago, 1874. Today, the American Kennel Club, which is an association composed of member clubs, some general and some specializing in one breed, sets the standards for the shows. The somewhat complicated point system used in judging dogs was set up by the AKC. Wherever *bona fide* dog shows are held, these rules and standards apply.

If your dog is properly registered with the American Kennel Club, he can be entered in a show. Check the papers or dog magazines for shows and write to the secretary of the show for the "premium list". Fill it in and send it back with the entry fee. You will then re-

Ch. Mueller Mills Valentino, owned by Mrs. Helen B. Case, has made a record of wins that will put him among the breed greats for all time. He is shown here winning a strong Sporting group at the Del Monte Kennel Club under Mr. Langdon Skarda. The handler of this magnificent Wirehair is Mr. Roy Murray.

Ch. Gretchenhof Moonshine, owned and bred by Gretchenhof Kennels, established wins that made her one of the top show dogs of the early sixties. Many times a best-in-show winner, she is seen here taking the top spot at the Golden Gate Kennel Club under judge Rutledge Gilliland, handler Walt Shallenbarger.

ceive your Exhibitor's Pass which will admit you and your dog.

There are five official classes:

Puppy Class: Open to dogs at least 6 months and not more than 12 months of age. This is limited to dogs whelped in the United States and Canada.

Novice Class: Open to dogs 6 months of age or older that have not won 3 first prizes at shows (wins in the puppy class are excepted). This is also limited to dogs whelped in the United States and Canada.

Bred by Exhibitor Class: This is open to all dogs except champions 6 months of age or older who are exhibited by the same person or kennel who was the recognized breeder on the records of the AKC.

American-bred Class: Open to dogs that are not champions, 6 months of age or over, whelped in the United States after a mating which took place in the United States.

Training the show dog must begin at a very tender age. The dog must learn to accept handling by strangers and should move with happy animation when he is gaited on the lead.

Open Class: This is open to dogs 6 months of age or over, with no exceptions. In addition, there are local classes, "special classes", and brace entries.

If you wish further information, see HOW TO SHOW YOUR OWN DOG by Virginia Tuck Nichols.

Chapter III

Heredity

Once upon a time there was a monk named Gregor Johann Mendel. And this monk had a pea patch. After some time he noticed that he could predict the appearance of his peas. He then began certain crossbreeding experiments and found that he could predetermine the growth of green peas or yellow peas, wrinkled peas or smooth peas, tall pea plants or short pea plants. From this ordinary pea garden he produced the beginnings of an extraordinary science—genetics. Mendel experimented with his peas and evolved the early theories of

The dog breeder must rely on a combination of living quality and pedigree study to produce the next generation of winners. Today's intelligent breeder considers a study of genetics as important as a knowledge of the Standard in order to keep bringing on dogs that win in the ring and excell in the field.

inheritance which so changed the course of biology, agriculture, medicine, and other related sciences. Of course, theories of heredity have progressed far beyond anything this simple monk could imagine, but it was his early experiments, unnoticed for many years, which helped touch off the revolution in the natural sciences.

Animal breeders were quick to use these theories in scientific breeding of purebred stock. Indeed, it is likely that many of them practiced it without knowledge of heredity. They bred like-to-like, bred dogs with favorable characteristics to obtain these traits in litters, and kept records of the matings for future reference. They crossbred different types of dogs to encourage new traits. If they did not know then what it was that transmitted the desired features, they did know that somehow they were passed on to the young.

Good kennel management knows that it is not enough to match up genes and chromosomes. This only transmits the raw material from

Ch. Horkseley Baron, owned by Mr. H. Booth.

Ch. Everserve Rolf, owned by Mr. I. Kono.

dog to dog. The environment must also be proper. No matter how beautiful a dog's coat could be, all his careful breeding will be lost if he isn't groomed and fed properly. Therefore modern breeders take advantage of modern science to breed scientifically, and then take care of the dogs which result from these matings.

THE THEORY OF INHERITANCE

There are many complex factors in inheritance, and modern geneticists are discovering more every day. Many things can influence the dog's breeding—but no outside interference can change his genetic structure, with the exception of accidental (or perhaps deliberate) mutation.

In all mammals we find two types of cells—soma and germ. The somatic cells make up every part of the organism but one—the germ

Ch. Adam V. Fuehrerheim, owned by Robert H. McKowen, embodies within himself the stamp of a many-faceted winner. His record includes no less than ten Specialty wins including the Parent Specialty. He has won over forty field trials and is the sire of numerous champions of bench and field.

Ch. Nevern Jagd Madchen, owned by Mr. R. H. Stevens.

plasm, which contains the germ cells. The germ plasm is the thin thread of our existence. All mammals, from the dog to man himself, are dependent on their germ plasm to perpetuate the species.

Germ plasm is found in mammals in the sperm of the male and eggs of the female. This substance contains tiny chemical entities called *genes*, which are contained in rod-like bodies called *Chromosomes*. Genes or groups of genes control the form and development of specific physical and mental characteristics. It may take several genes or combinations of genes to produce a certain appearance. For example, it may take any number of genes to control the appearance of your dog's coat. There are also genes to determine color, texture, length, curliness (or lack of it), and density of color. All of these factors can act together to produce the short, hard, liver and white coat of the Shorthaired Pointer or the hard, wiry coat of the Wirehaired Pointer.

Ch. Springfarm Ben of Cellerhof, owned by Mrs. S. M. Middleton.

The geneticist tells us that all the genes are found in every cell of the animal, *in pairs* (since the chromosomes also exist in pairs) everywhere but in the germ plasm. Even though every cell (other than the germ plasm) has a specialized function—skin, muscles, heart, eyes, etc., its nucleus still has within it the genetic "fingerprint" of the complete animal. When it reproduces itself in the process of *mitosis*, the fingerprint remains the same.

When the somatic cells are dividing and redividing during the formation of the new animal, they divide so that each chromosome is duplicated in the new cell. Thus each somatic cell receives the same pair of chromosomes, and consequently the same pairs of genes. The germ plasm cells divide in a different fashion. They also divide to form more cells, but each pair divides in half and either one half of the pair of chromosomes goes to each new cell. Germ cells therefore contain only one-half the necessary number of genes, because they contain only one-half the number of chromosomes. When the egg and sperm, each made up of these special germ cells with only

Each individual represents the genetic influence of sire and dam. In order to produce a desired result the breeder must know what the parent animals carry in dominant and recessive.

Ch. Nevern Jasper, owned by Sq. Ldr. D. W. Atkinson.

half the normal number of genes, unite, the genes again become paired. The new individual inherits half his genes from each parent, but we cannot tell which until he is born, although we can determine what kinds of characteristics he will inherit from the appearance and ancestry of his parents. Since many different combinations are possible, he will inherit different characteristics from his brothers and sisters—in fact, each individual is unique unto himself, although he resembles his species closely.

The important thing to remember is that each characteristic is determined by a pair of genes. How does this work? Why will two dogs with dark eyes, mated, produce a litter of dogs all with dark eyes, or a litter which has some dogs with light eyes?

There are two major types of genes—dominant and recessive. The dominant is the "stronger", you might say, and whenever it is present it overshadows the recessive or "weaker" gene. You can have a pair of genes with two dominant genes (purebred), two recessive genes (purebred), or a dominant and a recessive gene (hybrid). A charac-

Ch. Blitz of Longsutton, owned by Mr. J. Gassman.

teristic imparted by a recessive gene will show only if both genes are recessive; in other cases the dominant gene will determine the appearance of the particular characteristic.

Let us say that **D** represents the dominant dark color of the eye of the German Shorthair, and that **d** represents the lighter colored eye. Each dog has two such genes to determine eye color. Since dark is dominant over light, whenever there is a **D** gene present the dog's eyes will be dark in color. If he inherits a **D** gene from both his mother and father, he will pass only **D** genes to his children. But if the father with his **DD** mates with a bitch with **dd** genetic makeup (light eyes), the children will have dark eyes, but will be capable of transmitting light-eye genes. This means that if one of these children mates with another dog with either light eyes or some history of light eyes in the family, light eyes *can* appear in their children. Simple listings of the combinations possible will enable any dog owner to

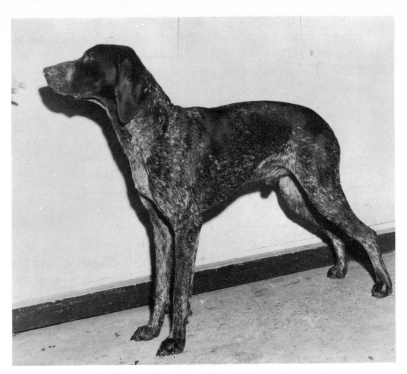

Ch. Larberry Link, owned by Miss J. A. Farrand.

see all the possible results of successive matings. It is by use of these Mendelian relations that dog breeders can control the quality of their dogs. Since light eyes are a fault, they can breed it out of the line by careful matings.

It is difficult to see these effects when you only produce a litter or two, but the following variations are possible. They become very real when many litters are produced or you have access to the records of many matings.

1. Two pure dark-eyed dogs when mated will produce only pure-bred dark-eyed dogs: **DD** x **DD** = **DD, DD, DD, DD.**

2. Two purebred light-eyed dogs when mated will produce only light-eyed dogs: **dd** x **dd** = **dd, dd, dd, dd.**

3. Two hybrids will produce some hybrids and some purebred dogs in the following ratios: **Dd** x **Dd** = **DD, Dd, Dd, dd.** This will show up as three dark-eyed dogs and one light-eyed dog.

4. A hybrid dark-eyed dog and a purebred dark-eyed dog will produce some purebred and some hybrid dogs, but all will have dark eyes: **DD** x **Dd** = **DD, Dd, DD, Dd.**

One way of illustrating how the gene theory works are boxes like the ones below:

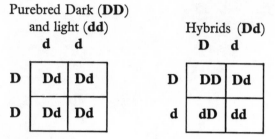

Purebred Dark (**DD**)
and light (**dd**)

Hybrids (**Dd**)

You cannot expect that in any single mating these ratios will show up, but once you have had many matings and litters you can see the patterns coming up. And since the theory is known, you need not take any chances. You can study the pedigrees and reported matings of both male and female dog and mate those which have characteristics you desire. If you mate a dog with dark eyes to a light-eyed dog, you may have some light-eyed animals in the litter, but since you know that light eyes are recessive, a dog with purebred genes for dark eyes mated with a light-eyed dog will produce dark-eyed dogs if you are sure there is no history of light-eyed dogs in his family. But if he carries the recessive gene, it may show up in the resulting litter.

Many people speak of a dog's bloodlines as if blood had something to do with inheritance. This is untrue. We should more properly talk of gene lines. Blood is just one physical factor determined by genes.

People also thought that influences on the mother dog while she was pregnant would mark the puppies. We even know of some persons who imagine that if the mother listens to music while she is pregnant, the child will have musical ability. Musical talent may run in the family, but this has nothing to do with listening to music during pregnancy.

MUTATIONS AND ABNORMALITIES

This brings us to the problem of changes in types. There are persons who believe that a dog whose coat is clipped will produce puppies having short coats. This is utter nonsense, as you can see by the genetic explanation. The length of a dog's coat is determined by

Ch. Blitzen Von Hackenschmidt, owned by Frank and Agnes Renninger and bred by John C. and Marjorie K. Schulte. A bitch of winning type, she has made a number of good wins and is of the sort that makes a desirable show star and producer. Her handler is Alvin E. Maurer, Jr.

his genetic makeup. Now if the breeder has been striving for a shorter coat, he can, using scientific methods, mate dogs which by chance have shorter coats than average. Inbreeding and line-breeding will then fix this characteristic, and dogs born of these matings will have shorter coats. In the case of the Shorthair, shorter coats were desirable and deliberately bred into the breed.

Occasionally there is a mutation in a breed. Genes are not immune to accident. Changes may be brought about chemically or from radiation (such as X-rays or nuclear radioactivity). Sometimes chromosomes "cross over", and this changes the genetic makeup. These changes are sudden and quite rare. If the breeder wishes to keep one of these mutant changes he can try to duplicate it with breeding, but most extreme mutations are downward on the evolutionary scale; only rarely is one an improvement.

Ch. Magdelen Drift, owned by Mr. K. Aspinall.

Ch. Seppl V. Donnaheim, owned by Dr. Herbert H. and Hannah Myers, and bred by Donald W. and Nancy P. Randall. Sire: Heinrich V. Donnaheim; dam: Ch. Randall's Spicecake. He is pictured with his handler, Jane K. Forsyth.

WAYS OF BREEDING

Using the knowledge of genetics or the old-time selective breeding, breeders are able to produce puppies which are almost perfect examples of their type. There are several ways of achieving this: in-breeding, line-breeding, out-breeding, and cross-breeding.

Inbreeding: You occasionally hear of "overbred" dogs. People will complain that too much inbreeding causes dogs to be temperamental or spoiled. Inbreeding itself doesn't cause this, but careless inbreed-ing does. Too many breeders are concerned only with how the puppy *looks*, not how he *acts*. So they breed for beauty only. If they ignore the fact that both parents were difficult dogs, overly sensitive, temperamental or nervous (and *tendencies* toward mental characteris-tics can be inherited), and mate these dogs because they are perfect specimens of their type, you may very well get a litter of overbred, oversensitive dogs.

Inbreeding, by mating dogs in the same immediate family, such as father to daughter, mother to son, or sister to brother, means doubling

Ch. Oldmill's Casanova, owned by Newton L. Compere was the first German Wirehaired Pointer to win a best in show in the United States. This he achieved at the Owensboro Kennel Club under Mr. Charles M. Siever. He was owner-shown to the win.

Ch. Zita Sand, owned by Mr. A. MacRae.

up on genes. If both the father and daughter have dark eyes, even if there are some light-eyed skeletons in the family closet, all the puppies will probably have dark eyes and there will be quite a few with **DD** as genetic makeup. If you then mate the father with one of his grand-daughters, you will add to the number of purebred dark-eyed dogs in the family. Brother and sister of the match can then be mated successfully. Of course, if undesirable characteristics show up in some of the matings, it would be wise to stop mating this particular pair of dogs and their offspring.

Inbreeding among animals is an accepted thing, if it is done carefully. Today such inbreeding, or incest, is forbidden among humans in almost every society. In the past tragic results occurred from human inbreeding: for example, the spread of inherited hemophilia as a result of inter-marriage in some European royal families.

Line-breeding: Line-breeding is mating dogs fairly closely related, keeping within the same family, but avoiding very close relatives. Cousins can be mated, for example. To establish a strain, dogs are usually bred with a combination of inbreeding and line-breeding. Inbreeding fixes certain desired traits, and line-breeding prevents undesirable traits from creeping in, but still keeps within the family. All modern breeds were inbred and line-bred, if you study their pedigrees.

Out-breeding: Out-breeding is mating dogs very distantly related, or possibly not related at all, although they must be pedigreed dogs in the same breed for the litter to be registered.

Cross-breeding: The thousands of mongrels you see are the results of cross-breeding, but it is not done by breeders, of course. There are times, however, when it is valuable. For example, we know that the German Shorthaired Pointer incorporates English Pointer traits for speed and Bloodhound traits for scenting ability. In the case of the German Wirehaired Pointer, it is probable that there is some

The genetic raw material represented by the young puppy must be brought along with great care by the breeder. Temperament must receive special care if the well-bred youngster is to successfully fill one of the many roles served by both the German Shorthaired and Wirehaired Pointers.

Ch. Adam's Happy Warrior, owned by Robert K. McKowen, and bred by Rudy Jordan. Sire: Ch. Adam V. Fuehrerheim; dam: Gretchenhof Tallyho. This eye-catching youngster is one of four champions in a single litter.

Schnauzer or Airedale mixed in, which gives him his distinctive coat. Both the Shorthaired and Wirehaired Pointer were extensively cross-bred by their German breeders in the early stages of their evolution.

HOW HEREDITY AFFECTS PHYSICAL CHARACTERISTICS AND BEHAVIOR

Mental Attitudes: Scientists and psychologists are still experimenting with animals to see just how an animal learns. Is a particular trait, such as scenting a trail, learned or inherited? The most we can say now is that certain tendencies run in families, and whether a pair of genes is directly responsible for this or not is not yet clear. Psychologists do know that if they take a family of rats, let us say, which are very good at finding their way through a maze, the children of the family will learn to find *their* way through the maze more quickly than rats from another, less talented family. If you take one of these talented rats away from its family and place it with another

In recent years, many new discoveries have been made in the areas of animal behavior. Those closest to this fascinating area know that the dam of a litter has a great deal of influence on the lifelong behavior patterns of her puppies.

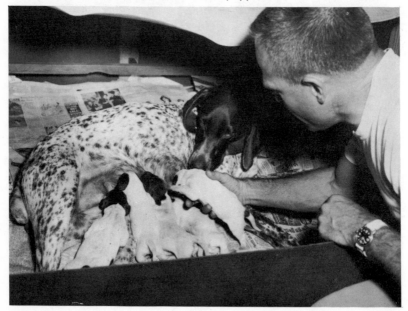

It has been proven that a puppy taken away from its mother and litter-mates at too early an age will not develop normally in later relations with its peers. Conversely, a puppy that is deprived of all human contact for the first twelve weeks of its life will revert to the wild and be entirely unapproachable. Behaviorists advise the best age to acquire a new puppy in view of the above is from seven to nine weeks.

family which is not as adept, it will not learn to get through the maze as rapidly, but if you put it back with its own family, it will learn more quickly than other rats might. Regardless of how a trait is acquired, however, family characteristics are important, as dog breeders have discovered through experience. Many examples are known.

Among all the bird-hunting breeds, the Spaniels are the only ones which are bred to keep their noses close to the ground, Hound fashion, when they hunt. Setters and Pointers hunt with heads high. In crosses of Cockers and Setters, the puppies all hunt with heads up, like Setters. Even in crosses of Setters with Bloodhounds, the progeny are useless as trailing dogs.. When you see a Cocker hunt with head carried high, you know that it probably has some inherited characteristics of English Setter in it. The high head is a dominant characteristic.

Some of the smaller breeds are natural tree dogs and make excellent squirrel dogs, but short coats are a necessity. Some Poodles, how-

Madresfield Hawthorn, owned and bred by Mr. Christopher Scott. This lovely English bitch is a winner of note, and has taken wins at the City of Birmingham and Irish Kennel Club shows. Sire: Ch. Larberry Link; dam: Madresfield Sitka Spruce.

Ch. Dunpender Weedenbrook Werra, owned by Mr. M. Bremder.

ever, tree almost as well as breeds bred for this, but this aptitude is not so well recognized as it should be by squirrel hunters.

While most persons never give posing a thought, observant breeders tell you how much easier it is to get some dogs to pose as show dogs than others. There are many who will stand in a show pose when no hand is on or under them. This characteristic seems to run in families. Of course, the "stand" can be taught, and all show dogs must learn to stand quietly when they are being judged.

Gun-shyness also seems to run in families. Many dogs are also thunder-shy. It would appear best not to breed them, although it is possible to train these dogs so that they are not a total loss for hunting or retrieving. It is also possible to ruin a perfectly fine hunting dog by the wrong approach to the noise of gunfire.

The tendency to piddle is another characteristic which appears to be inherited. Unfortunately it is often overlooked by breeders. There

It should go without saying that the genetic imprint of a good German Pointer should be the intrinsic desire and ability to hunt. There are many fine, dual-purpose dogs, available to breeders, who have these working qualities themselves and pass them along to their get, to the greater benefit of the entire fancy.

are too many dogs who panic and wet when strangers or even their masters approach. This is most discouraging if your dog is a house dog, and embarrassing if you wish to show him. It can be eliminated by careful breeding.

All typical retrieving breeds love to retrieve, but there are strains in which there is no interest; retrieving can be trained into these dogs only with great difficulty. On the other hand, you may see a leashed city-bred dog, familiar only with sparrows and pigeons, get out in a field and display a natural instinct for the art of retrieving. Careful breeding helps to preserve the hunting breeds and keep them from losing these instincts.

Natural retrievers seem to need something to carry around in their mouths. One of our friends came to visit with his dog, and the dog spent the entire afternoon carrying sticks of wood to the patio, until we had a considerable pile of winter firewood. We promptly invited our friend to come back again soon (with his dog) to complete the job.

Some retrievers may resort to picking up stools and carrying them around. If you keep some old tennis balls around you can discourage this filthy habit. You can also teach such dogs to fetch the paper or the mail or even carry something home in a bag.

Swimming is another characteristic that seems to be inherited, although the natural tendency has to be encouraged by parent dogs which swim or by the owner who encourages this sport. Water dog retrievers have to know how to swim, but there is great variation among families within breeds. If you want to hunt, and own a water-retrieving dog, or live near water, you will want a dog with this characteristic.

The tendency to contract disease may be inherited. We know that certain tendencies, such as heart trouble or length of life, run in human families. Back in the days when vaccines were not available and epidemics were rampant in animal families, dog owners noticed that certain breeds had different symptoms for some diseases, such as distemper. Cockers and Poodles, for example, did not have convulsions when their temperature started to rise. While this did not affect the mortality rates, it did make it harder to diagnose the disease in its early stages.

Since German Shorthaired and Wirehaired Pointers are used extensively for hunting, they must have scenting and retrieving abilities. They are bred for these characteristics as well as others, including water retrieving and endurance. It would appear wise to breed out dogs which shy at gunfire or are poor trackers or cannot stand staunchly to a point.

There is much to be learned in this fascinating field of genetics. Modern science has expanded and extended Mendel's simple ideas, and there is still much we can discover. We can predict the inheritance of physical characteristics such as color, shape, coat, skin, etc., although we cannot always be absolutely sure of the results. With so many factors to consider (such as color, size, coat) the possible variations are almost infinite in the more complex mammals. As for inheriting or acquiring mental characteristics such as temperament, hunting ability, and gun-shyness, there is considerable disagreement among animal psychologists, but the consensus seems to be that the tendency to learn or acquire these traits is most likely inherited, even though the traits themselves must be taught in some fashion.

Chapter IV

Inherited Characteristics

Mendel's theories of inheritance enabled him to predict the appearance of his garden peas. But, as we have seen, conclusions drawn from these early experiments have been elaborated and modified by modern scientists as more is known about the origin of life. For the more complex organisms such as the dog, many genetic factors may be responsible for any one characteristic.

COAT COLOR

Basic genetics tells us that we can predict that some if not all of the litter of two black-eyed Shorthairs will have dark eyes. The same theory which determines this can be applied to coat color and texture. But modern geneticists have discovered that the inheritance of coat color is not just the simple transmission of genes for black or genes for white. A number of genes determine coat color. There are different genes which will color your dog's coat, solid liver or liver and white ticked, or liver and white spotted and ticked or liver and white spotted or liver roan (a fine mixture of liver and white hair). Colors occasionally blend or change as a result of genetic mixing.

The ancient dog was a mixture of gray and brown, or derivations of black and yellow. All modern dogs have colorations which were originally possessed by their ancestors, passed down and modified by accidental or deliberate breeding.

The color and texture of the German Shorthair is carefully bred and maintained. The breed is young in years, and the type was probably set in the first 25 years of this century. Breeders know that the basic coat color is the result of the density of color pigments in the skin and hair. The denser the black pigments, the darker the coat color. Genes are responsible for this density. They also know that black is a dominant color gene, difficult to control once it has been bred into the line. Early in the development of the German Shorthair, breeders found that many of the dogs had light-colored eyes. In order

Ch. Callmac's Victory von Gardsburg, owned by H. R. and Shirley Hampton. This stylish bitch is shown scoring a nice win under the late Charles A. Schwarz, handler Bob Kelton.

to discourage this coloration, they bred the dogs with black Pointers, as they realized that black eyes were associated with black coats. A line of "Prussian Pointers" developed as a result, but breeders of Shorthairs took great care to breed out the black coat coloration while encouraging the darker eyes. There are still some of these black or gray Pointers, and they seem to be most useful in warmer climates, but the AKC standard for the German Shorthaired Pointer excludes black as a color.

The liver color is the result of a recessive brown gene and must be retained in purebred form (**bb**) in order to show up. Piebald dogs are recessive, but those with solid coats are not. Ticking is also a dominant gene, and there is some roan present as well.

The German Wirehaired Pointer has coloration similar to that of the Shorthair. However, he is rarely solid colored.

Ch. Dunpender Brian, owned by Mr. A. Macrae.

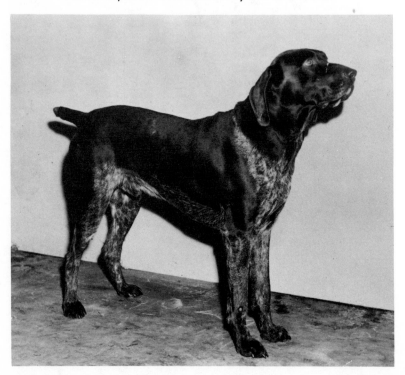

Ch. Mueller Mills Valentino II, owned by Mrs. Helen B. Case. This handsome son of Ch. Mueller Mills Valentino finished his championship in noteworthy style at the tender age of eight months. His handler, Evonne Chashoudian, looks on.

COAT TEXTURE

The coat texture of both the Wirehaired and Shorthaired Pointer is very important. The waterproof quality is one of the essential features of both. Both dogs can retrieve in water, and their coats dry quickly. The Shorthair has a short, dense, hard outer coat which dries very quickly. A very short, dense, waterproof, oily undercoat was also bred in. One reason for the undercoat is that German breeders bred it into the breed in order to retain the short outer coat and prevent it from lengthening.

The coat texture of the Wirehaired Pointer is equally important to the hunter, but as yet there is still considerable variation in appearance. Some almost resemble the Shorthairs; others are or could be

Ch. Adam V. Fuehrerheim, owned and shown by Robert K. McKowen taking the top prize in one of the ten specialties he has to his credit. This one is the Finger Lakes Club and the judge here was Mr. Alfred J. Sause.

Ch. Mordax Morning Mist, owned by Miss J. A. Farrand.

mistaken for the fuzzier Griffon. The coat is especially adapted for water work or rough land cover. On the other hand, it is also more prone to pick up burrs and dirt. Breeders are working hard to stabilize the texture of the Wirehair's coat.

SIZE

The AKC Standards specify that Shorthaired Pointers should be between 21 and 25 inches tall, depending on the sex, and most Wirehairs are between 22 and 26 inches high. While these dogs are not the largest in dogdom, their size is ideal for the hunter or house-owner. We do not use these Pointers for large game in this country, but they can hunt rabbit, duck and other types of game.

Their size makes them easily seen in the field, and they can retrieve most game easily. But their size is also an asset at home, where they are excellent watchdogs and companions. No dog likes to be mauled, but when there are children in the household, a dog the size of the Pointer can join in the games and fend for himself without being injured.

TEMPERAMENT

Animal behaviorists and geneticists are not sure whether certain traits of behavior characteristics are inherited or not, and this is still being investigated. We do know that the best of dogs (from a genetic standpoint) can be ruined by improper training and care, and a relatively unpromising dog can become a faithful and loving pet if he is treated well.

The Pointer points—this is an indisputable fact. When you put a pup in the field he will chase the butterflies and flush birds, but every so often he will stiffen into a genuine point, without training of any sort. In most cases this is the result of that moment of hesitation just before he springs. This characteristic is encouraged by breeders, but it must be trained and disciplined to develop properly. Pointers are judged by their ability to point "staunchly"—that is, to hold the point without a break and with the proper stance. Of course, when dogs are being tested on planted birds, they cannot be expected to hold as staunchly, as the man-scent is on the birds.

The German Shorthair also retrieves, another characteristic which must be encouraged, although they will naturally pick up and carry a dead bird or other objects. The Pointer's superior ability to scent and trail game is the result of his Bloodhound ancestry. While he is slower than some other breeds, his slowness aids him in hunting pheasant when the scent is faint. His fine nose also helps him to trail wounded animals.

One of the chief qualities of both Wirehaired and Shorthaired Pointers is their trainability. These dogs are easily taught, and they can learn by watching other dogs in the field. This easy temperament makes them excellent pets as well.

The most difficult trait to be instilled in the hunting dog is to hold his point—he must not break at the sound of the gun nor break to flush the birds. He must return when called, but he must also be free enough to range far without constant reminders from his master.

Discipline is sometimes a problem. The Shorthair is an active, energetic dog. He needs to be occupied and running much of the

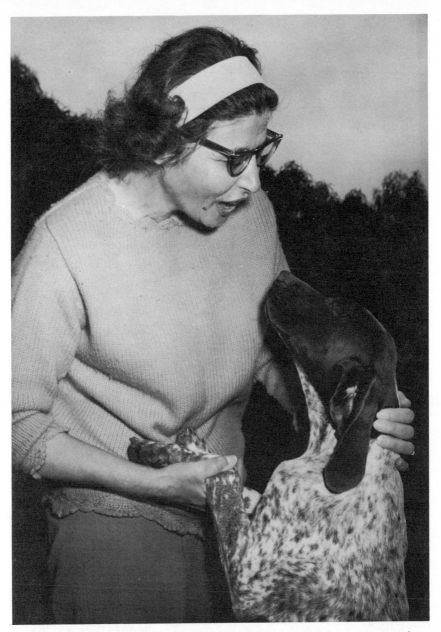

Both German Pointers have been bred for amiable dispositions and temperament that would be receptive to training. No dog who does not reflect this kindly breed nature should be considered as a pet, show dog, hunting companion or breeding animal.

Those that fashioned the German Pointers in the beginning strove for a dog that was useful in field and a source of pleasure in the home. The fanciers of today have kept these features intact, and these dogs still stand ready to give completely of themselves for the benefit of their human families.

time. He wants a firm but kindly hand as well as love and attention. We have seen a friend's Shorthair who just loves to climb in his mistress's lap, and she doesn't mind it a bit—except when she is in a bathing suit!

The Wirehair is somewhat less of a discipline problem, as he is "softer" than most Shorthairs. But he still needs lots of activity and exercise and loves nothing more than learning new tricks or following his master in the field. He can cozen most dog lovers and even those indifferent to dogs into attention and affection.

Both the Shorthair and Wirehair have been carefully bred for their hunting ability (a nose for pointing, retrieving ability; range and agility in the field), and these characteristics have been encouraged by scrupulous breeders. In addition, they are easily trained and are tractable and loving family dogs. All of these qualities, properly instilled, make the German Shorthair and Wirehair ideal hunting dogs for the hunter who wants only one dog, and a fine addition to the family hearth and home.

APPEARANCE

In appearance, the Shorthair is of medium height, powerful and agile. His head is clean cut with a long muzzle, and strong jaws (for retrieving). When he runs, his compact, well knit body gaits at a smooth pace. Both Pointers have docked tails. In most breeds, the tails are docked for a reason, not just appearance. The Pointer's docked tail is protected from chaffing and injury in the field.

The Wirehair is not so sturdy as the Shorthair—he is rather slender and agile, and his size helps him set a fast, medium-ranging pace. In addition, he has the facial features of most wirehaired breeds, the heavy eyebrows, beard and whiskers, creating an impression of liveliness and humor.

Because both of these dogs are fairly recent in dog history, (although their ancestors go back to the Middle Ages), there are occasional variations in type. As noted before, Shorthairs are sometimes houndy in appearance, heavy and slow moving. This has been modified considerably in America, where speed and range are important. Time will undoubtedly "set" desirable characteristics more permanently, but only if aided by careful, controlled breeding.

LIFE SPAN

Most dogs live to a ripe old age if given proper care. The Methuselahs of the dog world may even reach 18 or 20 years of age, although 12 or 14 is about average. Hunting dogs are prone to accident, but even at 8 and 10 years of age they can be useful hunters.

Chapter V

Reproduction

Would you like to raise a litter of puppies? Even if you purchased your pet with no intention of breeding, there may come a time when you would like to see its offspring. Or, as is often the case, despite all your precautions, someone has gotten into the barn and stolen the horse, and your dog is pregnant, the sire unknown.

Breeding raises many problems for the novice, and we suggest that you familiarize yourself with Chapter III, the principles of heredity, before you undertake to breed.

CONTRACTS

If you are planning to breed a litter, your best bet is to go to a professional kennel and arrange for a stud (male dog). Be prepared, however, for making contractual arrangements, and the authors believe that if large amounts of money or complicated arrangements are involved, you should have your lawyer check the contract. In general, there are two types of fees. Most kennels charge a fee for the use of a stud. This may vary from $25 to $200, depending on the dog. If the stud is a famous champion, the cost will be higher. The other type of contract is written so that the owner of the stud gets the pick of the litter. In this case, the breeder has first choice of a puppy or puppies. Be sure that all contingencies are spelled out. In most contracts, if your bitch fails to be impregnated the first time, you can rebreed her with the same dog when she is next in heat for no extra charge. This is called a *return service*.

THE BITCH

A little friend of ours always talks about when his dog is "heating",

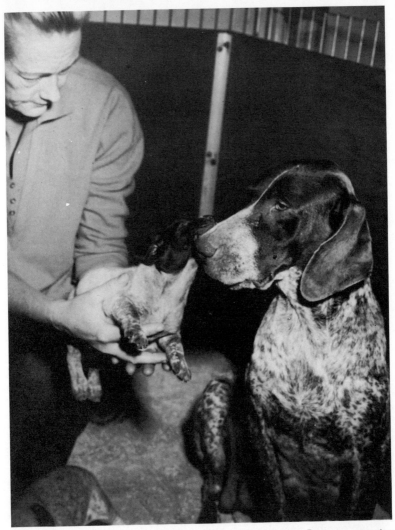

Whoever contemplates breeding a litter of German Pointer puppies should determine beforehand what the breeding is to accomplish. Every litter bred should be brought about for a specific reason whether the breeder wants puppies for the field, bench or anything else he should make sure the puppies live up to his own expectations.

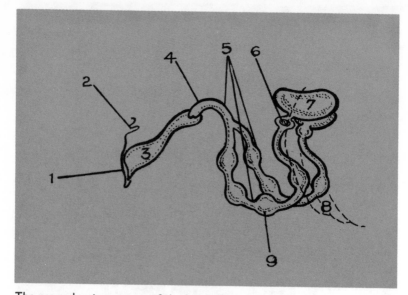

The reproductive system of the bitch: 1. vulva, 2. anus, 3. vagina, 4. cervix, 5. uterus, 6. ovary, 7. kidneys, 8. ribs, 9. fetal lump.

much to our amusement. But he does understand something about the reproductive process and we feel that this is important. This is an excellent way to explain to children, in as much or as little detail as you wish, the way dogs (and people) are "made." It is certainly far more reliable than the information picked up on street corners from uninformed children.

Dogs, like people, ovulate rhythmically, excepting that where humans ovulate 13 times a year, dogs only come into heat (i.e. ovulate) twice a year. All mammals have the same type of reproductive organs, and although they are not alike in appearance they work in the same manner.

REPRODUCTIVE ORGANS (BITCH)

The female ovaries are located in the abdomen, high behind the ribs. Each ovary is encircled by a capsule with a slit on one side. The capsule is surrounded by spongy tissues known as the *fimbria*. Starting at the slit of each ovary are the *Fallopian tubes*, two tiny tubes which run a zigzag course over each capsule and terminate at the upper end of one of the branches of the Y-shaped *uterus*. The diagram above shows the reproductive system of the bitch. Note that the uterus which is long and Y-shaped is different from the shape of the human uterus.

The eggs in the ovaries contain germ plasm, that unique bit of matter which determines your dog's inheritance and assures the continuance of the breed. When the eggs mature, they ripen in blister-like pockets which grow towards the surface of the ovaries. These pockets, called *follicles*, produce a follicular hormone which prepares the uterus. The walls of the pockets are thin and eventually burst, liberating the eggs into the capsule surrounding the ovaries, and they move into the Fallopian tubes and are ready for fertilization. Your dog is "heating."

When one contemplates a breeding, the stud should be selected and his service reserved well in advance. When the owner has observed that the bitch is in season she should be shipped to the stud (if necessary) in time for her to become accustomed to the new environment before the breeding is accomplished.

Ch. Hager V. Feuhrerheim, owned by Alvin E. Maurer, Jr. and bred by Harold G. Feuhrer. Sire: Ch. Baron V. Feuhrerheim; dam: Bellaire Heidie. He is shown with his owner-handler after scoring winners dog at the Westminster Kennel Club.

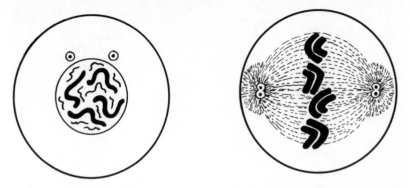

Two steps in the process of mitosis. This is the phenomenon of cell division that takes place upon the union of sperm and egg cell. This cell division continues throughout the period of gestation until the new life comes into being.

When copulation occurs (the mating of the bitch with the male dog), sperm are transferred from the male to the female and are moved up the uterus by the same sort of movement (peristalsis) that occurs in the intestines. Within a few minutes of tieing (mating) the sperm are already up in the uterus, through the tubes, and in the capsule surrounding the ovaries.

It takes many sperm to help fertilize one egg; the sperm has an enzyme which breaks down the egg's resistance until one sperm enters. Only one is needed for *fertilization*, and as soon as this sperm has entered the egg, the egg changes and becomes impervious to other sperm.

The eggs, fertilized or not, move down through the Fallopian tubes into the uterus and there, if fertilized, become attached to the uterine lining (endometrium) and grow. Oftentimes, they are not fertilized in the capsule, but meet the sperm in their travels to the uterus and are fertilized and then nest in the uterus. The chromosomes in the egg and the sperm unite, making a complete set. The fertilized egg divides six times, each cell containing the same chromosomes, and at the sixth division one pair of cells are formed which become the germ plasm of the pup. The dividing cells form a hollow globe, which finally pulls in on one side, as if you let the air out of a

Sh. Ch. Decima, owned by Maj. Gen. and Mrs. P. H. de Havilland.

hollow rubber ball and pushed one side of it in until it touched the other side. If you then squeezed the ball together until you made a canoe-shaped body, and continued squeezing until the two gunwales touched and stayed closed, you would duplicate the process of cell division in the egg.

By the twenty-second day the foetus (unborn puppy) is a very tiny object which is surrounded by protective coverings (the sac) and the placenta which is a band of flesh connecting the foetus with the uterus. At this point, if you put your thumb and fingers on each side of the bitch's belly, you will feel the tiny marble-like lumps which are puppies. These grow and by the twenty-fourth day they are larger and continue to grow until you can't distinguish the individual puppies, as the lumps are so soft. By this time, your dog, however, looks pregnant, as just a glance at her size will tell you.

THE OVULATION CYCLE

As we have already said, ovulation is a rhythmic cycle occurring twice a year, about once every six months. Scientists believe that the changing length of the day is the chief influence inducing the cycle which makes the reproduction possible. As the days grow shorter in late summer and longer in late winter, most bitches come into heat.

This fact can be used to bring the bitch into heat artificially by the use of artificial light. If the length of her day is increased by light, one hour the first week, two the second, three the third, and four the fourth, she can be brought into heat by the end of the fourth week. Even shipping a bitch from one part of the country to the other, where the days have different lengths, can change her cycle. Be careful, therefore, if you move your dog from Maine to Georgia; you may find yourself with a bitch ready for mating.

A more certain method of bringing the bitch into heat artificially is the use of drugs such as stilbestrol, which encourages ovulation.

THE MATURE CYCLE

A female's cycle is made up of four parts; the *proestrum*, the *estrum*, the *anestrum*, and the *metestrum*. She will ovulate during a three-week period and the manner in which this occurs makes it possible for you to quickly get your dog under cover or plan for mating.

The first signs of ovulation, the period of *proestrum*, are an enlarged and swollen vulva and a bloody discharge. The follicles, which hold the eggs, are rupturing, and forming bloody plugs (pits) called blood bodies (*corpora hemorrhagica*) which soon change and secrete a hormone called the *luteal hormone*. The blood bodies become quite tough and are now called *luteal bodies*. This hormone brakes the mating cycle and at this point the dog enters the *estrum* period. Up to now she has not been interested in males. But they are interested in her! She is restless, her appetite may increase and she has the physical symptoms listed above. Now her vulva loses its firmness and within 36 hours becomes flabby and soft. The color of the discharge changes and becomes paler. By the second week your bitch is ready to accept the male and his advances. The eggs are not ready for fertilization before the middle of the acceptance period, however, and since the sperm can only live about three days in the female, you should not mate her before the 10th day after the first signs of discharge, close to ovulation, either a day before or any time during the rest of the period of estrum.

The next two months are called the *anestrum* and the next three the *metestrum*, being the five month period when the bitch is not in heat. After this she's ready to begin again.

If you do not wish to mate your dog, you have only one problem—keeping her from getting pregnant. The careful dog owner will either send his dog to a kennel until ovulation is over, or keep the dog in the house and on a leash when outside. Even so, the male dogs will collect from all corners. It seems that the urine of a dog about to come into heat has a peculiar odor which attracts male dogs. Many dogs, when walked on the leash, are taken far from home so that the urine odor is not present around the house. If you live in an apartment, you can purchase a belt in the pet store which will protect your dog and also your rugs.

MATING THE BITCH

Suppose you have decided to have a litter of Pointer pups. When and how should you arrange for this? Your dog matures at about 8 months or more. Some dogs, especially large breeds or toys,

NORMAL BITCH MATING CYCLE

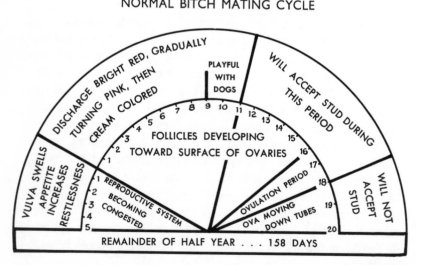

Most authorities on the subject consider it best not to breed a bitch on her first season, but rather to wait until she is more mature. In this way she is physically and temperamentally more equal to the task.

ovulate for the first time as late as twelve months or more. Are they ready for breeding? Some breeders say no, that they are not ready, are not mature enough to care for puppies. However, there are many compelling reasons for mating your dog as soon as you can. For one thing, it is easier for a young dog with flexible bones to bear her puppies than an older one. The puppies will be just as good as ones bred later on in life. The bitch can certainly take care of her puppies. Nature provides hormones to aid her. And if she seems awkward with the first litter, this is merely inexperience and she will improve with her next litters. Just think how most new mothers feel about their first child and how awkward each operation like bathing and dressing seems. By the second, things are much easier.

Another excellent reason for early breeding is preserving the blood lines. After all, many accidents can happen to dogs as they grow older and if you have bred your bitch and obtained a litter of puppies, you have sons and daughters to carry on the "family name." Many professional breeders breed early to ascertain which dogs are the best breeders.

When your dog is ready for breeding, be sure she is in good health. If your bitch is a virgin, you should have an experienced male dog. The virgin may be nervous or jumpy and an equally new stud will only make it worse. The experienced dog knows just what to do and is efficient and calm. Many people send their dog to the kennel and come and collect her when it is all over. But often your presence is required, especially if she is nervous. Generally, your dog is mated two or perhaps three times, once a day, and then sent home. You may have to help. If she refuses to permit copulation you will have to hold her up with your hand under her shoulders or, if she is a large dog, with your knee. If she is snappish, a muzzle is required. Once the dogs are "tied," then the stud will be gently turned, and the period of copulation will last from several minutes to several hours. The reasons for this will be explained later, in the section on the male dog.

After mating it is advised that you keep the female quiet, and she may be serviced again the next day. Obviously, you must be sure that no other dogs get to her after this mating, for if she has not been impregnated the first time, you may end up with a litter of puppies, father unknown. If the mating has taken, you will become the proud owner of a litter of pups about 63 days later.

SPAYING

Suppose that you have a female dog and don't wish to mate her. You may not want to go through the bother and expense of kenneling her when she is in heat or the nuisance of the collection of amorous male dogs outside your door. A bitch can best be spayed before her first heat, at about five months. This is accomplished by a surgical operation called a hysterectomy, when the sexual organs are removed. Many people say that a spayed dog becomes fat and lazy, but this need not be true. If you regulate your dog's diet and see that she gets enough exercise, she will probably remain fairly normal in size.

REPRODUCTION IN THE MALE

Most male dogs can be bred from about the age of a year until they are quite old. Some oldsters of 10 years or more have been known as perfectly fine studs. Handlers feel that a good stud can

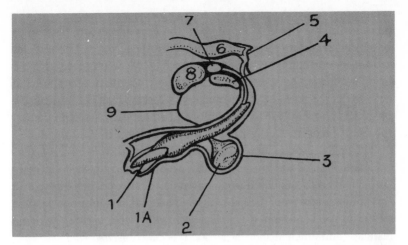

The reproductive system of the dog: 1a. sheath, 1. penis, 2. testicle, 3. scrotum, 4. pelvic bone, 5. anus, 6. rectum, 7. prostate, 8. bladder, 9. vas deferens.

be mated several times a week for several weeks in succession, but then a rest is in order. Of course, his health must be maintained, the diet good, and condition tip-top. If you own a male and wish to mate him, perhaps for a puppy or two, you will find it more difficult. Most breeders have their own studs and are looking for females. But you may be fortunate to find a breeder or an individual with a female dog he wishes to mate to a dog of your male's characteristics. Again, be sure the contract is properly checked.

REPRODUCTIVE ORGANS (MALE)

The sperm in the male dog are tiny bodies shaped like polliwogs. They are oval and flattish, with a tail about nine times the size of the body. Each sperm has half the necessary number of chromosomes. But there is one important difference between male sperm and female eggs. The male sperm determines the sex of the puppy. There are two different types of sex chromosomes in the sperm, one the **X** and the other the **Y**. The egg contains only **X** chromosomes. When a **X** and a **X** unite, the result is a female puppy, when the **X** and the **Y** unite, you have a male puppy.

The sperm are manufactured in the testicles by the germ plasm. The development of the dog's genitals follows a regular course as in other mammals. During puberty, the testicles, which form inside the body, descend into a loose sac. They are attached to the peritoneum and grow down through the abdominal slits (known as rings) and drop into the sac, which is called the *scrotum*. The testicles are outside the body, as the warmth of the body can interfere with the manufacture of the sperm. But nature sees that they are protected against the weather and other dangers. When it is very cold a muscle pulls the testicles close to the body, and when warm weather comes, the muscle loosens so that the air can cool them.

If a dog's testicles fail to descend the condition is called *cryptorchidism*. Use of the hormone APL, administered by the veterinarian, can correct this condition, but it is considered hereditary and this might make your dog an unpopular stud. If only one testicle descends the condition is called *monorchidism* and the dog with no testicles (and no chance of fatherhood) is called an *anorchid*.

The dog's penis is unique in that it contains a bone in the front part which aids the dog to achieve copulation. In addition, besides being capable of enlarging with blood, the penis also has an area which enlarges much more than the forepart does. When the male mates with a female dog, his penis swells and the bulbous part becomes at least three times the size of the rest of the penis. This prevents the penis from slipping out during copulation, at which time the dogs are "tied."

When tieing has occured, the semen is pumped in spurts into the vagina. Rhythmic waves which tighten and relax the vagina help also. Some males remain tied five minutes, others an hour or longer. But a five-minute tie can be just as satisfactory, as the semen have moved up through the uterus and tubes to the ovaries by that time.

THE STUD

If your dog is inexperienced, it is best to mate him when he is about a year old to an experienced female. You may have to push him towards her or even force him. Be sure that the bitch does not snap or bite at him. Occasionally, the dogs may have difficulty mating, especially if they are of different sizes. If you are not experienced, it is best to have the assistance of a knowledgeable handler. He will know all the tricks of the trade and insure a successful mating. The first two or three services are very important and unless they are properly handled, your dog may have trouble mating in the future.

After the first service, the dogs will be rested. If the male is young and not too successful the first time, the handler may let him try again in a few hours. For a new dog, it is best to have a bitch just coming into heat, so that by the time the male is more used to her and experienced, she will not have passed her ovulation period.

Will you injure your dog if you don't mate him? Or will he be oversexed if he is mated often? Most breeders say no. They do feel that it is unwise to start to mate your dog after he is four years old. By this time it is too late to accustom him to the problems of fatherhood. But most unpenned dogs will roam, and will react to the female in heat. If your dog is not kept penned, the chances are that he will find a stray female somewhere. If you wish your dog to be a good stud, it is wise not to let him roam. As you have seen, it is difficult to train the young male to be a good stud. Allow him to mate only with proper dogs, under proper conditions where there is little chance of injury, and he will retain his value as a stud. By keeping a record of your dog's offspring, you will be able to determine in advance what kind of puppies will result from matings with a particular type of bitch.

Chapter VI

Pregnancy and Motherhood

INTRODUCTION

You are about to have puppies . . . or rather your dog is. The first rule is to RELAX; take some time to talk to your veterinarian about prenatal and whelping care, then sit back and wait 63 days from the day of breeding. Mark on your calendar the expected date—plus or minus a day or two—and prepare yourself. When the expected date rolls around, stay home. One friend of ours left the house in care of a babysitter and came home to find that the sitter had been midwife for 8 puppies—surely above and beyond the call of duty!

PREGNANCY

One of the problems of canine pregnancy is that we sometimes don't know if the dog is pregnant for several weeks after breeding. Rabbit tests for dogs do not exist. Some bitches, even though not pregnant, will exhibit symptoms of pregnancy, which can be misleading and disappointing, if you are hoping for a litter of pups. True pregnancy is unmistakable by around the fifth or sixth week, for the abdomen swells slightly, and the nipples become red and puffy. By the 35th day your veterinarian can eliminate any lingering doubts by a thorough examination. It is at this time he should give you dietary instructions, if any, and other relevant information.

Should your dog be pregnant, both you and the expectant mother will prepare. Nature provides for pregnant mothers by releasing hormones which increase maternal instincts, as well as the hormones which start labor and milk production. But since our dogs are a part of us and we are responsible for their care, we can also help them through this period.

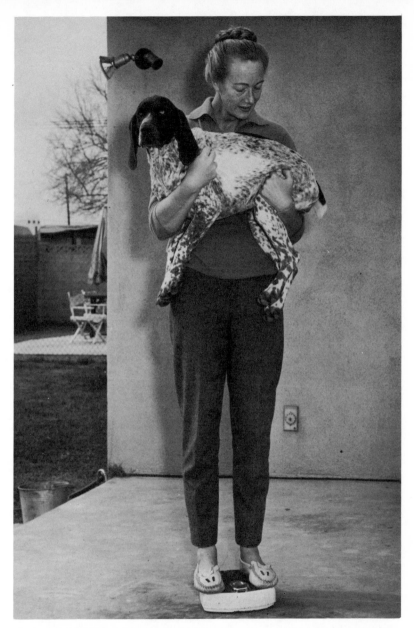

One method of determining whether or not a bred bitch is in whelp is to take weekly weight checks after about the fourth or fifth week of pregnancy. This is not necessarily an indication of the size of the litter, but only a pointer that one is on its way.

During the first weeks of pregnancy a bitch may be given her normal exercise, but as the time for the arrival of the litter draws nearer strenuous activity should be avoided.

A pregnant bitch requires more food, but should not be overfed. Divide the meals into two, and supplement them with milk and biscuits in the middle of the day. Additional vitamins, A & D, may be advised and 2 to 4 teaspoons given daily is usually the rule depending on the size of the dog. Just before whelping time most dogs cut down on their food. There just isn't room for both the litter and meal. But see that she continues to eat something, especially light meals with meat and milk. You can encourage feeding by giving her favorite foods. In general, dogs thrive on high protein diets during pregnancy and if you have been feeding your dog her usual excellent diet, she should do well.

You must be sure she is exercised, *but* not too violently or under duress. Short-legged dogs should be kept from too much stair climbing and you should try to keep your dog from excited jumping up and down off beds and chairs, or roughhousing with children. One of the problems of pregnancy is constipation, and regular, sensible exercise as well as a good diet will help. You may have to use mineral oil as well to help alleviate this condition.

Some doctors advocate worming around the third or fourth week. It would be best to check with your veterinarian, in any event, because he should prescribe the dosage or, even better, do the worming himself.

If your dog is Wirehaired, you can make it easier for the pups to nurse by trimming the hair around the nipples when she is almost ready to whelp. This helps prevent worm infestations and lost puppies.

In days past, before dog became man's best friend, a pregnant bitch, about to whelp, would make a nest. She might scratch a hole in the ground and root around until it was soft and comfortable. But nowadays dogs live in our houses or around them, and we are responsible for a dog's "maternity room." A whelping box is easy to make and maintain. Some people give over the whole matter to the veterinarian and have the whelp at his hospital or a professional

Under normal circumstances a bitch is quite capable of seeing to the birth of her litter without assistance. It is considered to be a wise precaution, however, that someone familiar to her be there when her whelps come into the world in case some form of human assistance becomes required.

kennel with facilities. But most of us want to be near our dog when she whelps and may also want our families to watch. It is a wonderful way to introduce children to the marvels of motherhood, in a wholesome, natural way. You must, however, be sure that the spectators are instructed not to disturb the mother or pups during labor.

The whelping box is a low sided box which is roomy enough for the mother and puppies. If you have a big dog, be sure it is large enough, at least four feet square with sides one foot high. Your local pet supplier may be able to help you with your selection of a whelping box, but should a supplier be unavailable a homemade box can be constructed of wood with an additional one-inch ledge around the inside, in case your dog is an awkward mother with a tendency to sit on her offspring. One side should be hinged so that you may clean it easily.

Even a large cardboard box will do. Cover the bottom of your box with a piece of linoleum and then a thick wad of newspapers. Do not use rags; they are dangerous and puppies can smother under them.

Where conditions warrant it often helps to have a portable heater for the greater comfort of the dam and her litter.

Where do you put the whelping box? Probably the best place is the warm kitchen, but this may not be large enough or convenient for your family. Some dogs, especially larger ones, are happier in an out-of-way place. Any room which is warm and free from drafts will do. A cellar, unless it is very warm and dry, is not suitable. Besides the physical danger to mother and pups, you will spend your days going up and down stairs to attend to their needs. You want to be where you can see that all those wiggling balls of fur are not getting into trouble, in or out of the box.

Most dogs are used to their own beds or kennels. Be sure that you accustom your dog to her "maternity room," or you may find her whelping in a closet corner among the shoes or out in the garden under a bush.

But most of all, see that you have a peaceful home. You can forgive your dog an occasional upset stomach or indigestion. After all, there's no morning sickness or maternity clothes and the hospital bills are low. Maternity is a natural function of dogs and under happy, peaceful conditions, your dog can be expected to care for herself with little or no problem, requiring only a minimum of sympathetic assistance from you.

WHELPING

You have provided the whelping box, and the mother-to-be has been carefully fed and exercised, and examined by the veterinarian. Now you have your eye on the calendar. Perhaps you have an arrangement to bring your dog to the veterinarian when labor begins, or he is to come to the house. Your dog may start in the middle of the night, when you can't get help easily. Remember, if there is any trouble at all, call your veterinarian, regardless of the hour. A dog, whether she is a valuable show dog or a beloved family pet, deserves professional help if she cannot help herself.

Most dogs, however, bear their young easily. Certain breeds, because of selective breeding, may have had basic body changes, and whelping is difficult. Such difficulty is predictable and your veterinarian's advice will enable you to help the mother over the rough spots. Occasionally, a Caesarian is recommended. Reliable doctors will not suggest an operation unless it is an absolute necessity, because of danger to the mother and the problems of aftercare for the pups.

Be prepared should be our motto. Here is a list of things you can have ready when your dog is about to whelp: the whelping box, lined with newspaper, extra newspaper, towels, cotton, warm water, a scissors to cut the cord, thread to tie the cord, an electric heating pad or hotwater bottles, an eye dropper in case you have to feed the puppies, and if you happen to have them, a pair of scales to weigh the puppies as they are born. It is a good idea, especially if your puppies are pure-bred, to have a pad of paper and pencil to record markings, weight, time of arrival, etc., of each puppy.

How do you know when the event is about to begin? Your dog's behavior will tell you. She will start preparing a "nest," just as if you hadn't provided one for her. All those carefully arranged papers which you put in the whelping box will be torn up and arranged and rearranged. This is her first maternal act—making a home for her puppies. She will look distracted, restless, anxious, and start to pant. Probably, her last meal will be untouched or she may have some indigestion.

After all of the puppies have been born and the bitch is at her ease with them, the owner should examine each to determine sex, color and markings, and whether or not any congenital deformities are present.

If you have taken her temperature before all these symptoms appear, it will be around normal, 101.5°. About 12 hours before labor begins, it drops radically to 97° or 98°. This is a sure sign. If it shoots up again, better call the doctor . . . something may be wrong!

Real contractions are unmistakable. The dog will tense, hunch up, strain, relax. This is repeated over and over as she settles down to business. The contractions are widening the mouth of the womb and pushing the sac containing the first puppy towards the cervix, which is in the pelvis, now widening to receive this precious package. This is one reason for not allowing older dogs to breed for the first time. The bone and cartilage in the pelvic area harden as the dog grows older and cannot stretch during labor. If true contractions continue more than three or four hours without success, you had better call the veterinarian. This means that there is some problem with the bitch or foetus and delay may mean injury to your dog and the loss of the litter.

If your dog has trouble actually pushing her puppy out, you may be called upon as an assistant obstetrician. The most important things to remember are: *never* put your fingers into the dog's vagina, and *never* force the puppy out, in any way. The best way you can aid your dog is, using a towel, hold onto the sac containing the puppy and gently apply traction to the puppy as it comes out with the contractions. This is only to prevent it from slipping back into the mother. Exert *no* pull at all. Once the puppy is out, a slight tug on the cord will help bring the placenta out too. If it looks as though your dog is having trouble whelping, call the veterinarian.

Whelping takes from 1 to 12 hours but an average litter of 4-5 puppies generally takes about 4 hours. Some take longer. And the puppies can arrive from 5 to 60 minutes apart. In between puppies, take your dog outside to relieve herself or even give her a little milk. But if she is not done whelping she will remain restless and continue straining.

Most puppies come into the world head first, although there are quite a number which make their debut feet first. Sometimes the puppy is preceded by a rush of water as the sac breaks, but more often it is born with the sac intact. The foetus develops in a sac filled with liquid. Each sac is attached to the mother by a band of flesh called the *placenta*. The umbilical cord connects the foetus and the placenta and nourishment from the mother is sent to the puppy

Healthy puppies are quiet puppies. Until their eyes open your puppies will do little more than eat and sleep. Constant crying should be investigated as this might indicate something is wrong with the puppies or, possibly, the dam's milk supply.

through the cord. When the puppy is born, if the sac is still around it, the mother dog, her maternal instincts all working, will tear the sac off, cut the cord, and she will often eat the sac, cord, and placenta which follows it. Nowadays, it seems there are some lazy dogs, and their masters must help them whelp, or perhaps the puppies are arriving at such a rate that she has no time. If your dog cannot aid the puppy, or is too distracted with the next arrival, your help is essential. Break the sac and strip it back over the puppy. Cut the cord about 1-2″ from the navel and, if advised to do so by your veterinarian, tie the cord with a bit of silk string. Some doctors feel that the mother may worry over the string and nibble at it, causing infection. In most cases, there is little or no bleeding through the umbilical cord. The cord dries up and drops off in a few days.

When a puppy emerges, and the mother has stripped off the covering, she will lick and lick it and tumble it about until it is breathing normally, dry, moving and squealing. Sometimes she cannot do this, or the puppy may not start to breathe. Immediately take up the dog in a towel and massage it vigorously. Don't be afraid, you won't injure it. You may even hold it upside down and shake it to clear the lungs. If it still doesn't respond, artificial respiration is next. One method is to breathe into the dog's mouth until the lungs are filled and breathing starts. Or you can hold the dog with the navel away from you, grasp the cord with thumb and pinky and alternately pull the cord and press against his chest with the other three fingers. A third method is to raise and lower the legs rhythmically against the dog's chest. *Don't give up, your chances of success are good.* This often happens when the dog arrives feet first and the cord is pinched or cut before he is out; other pups may arrive this way, so you had better call the veterinarian if you need help.

With a large dog and a large litter, you may want to provide a temporary nursery. A dog in hard labor may throw herself about and her helpless newborn pups can be crushed. Place a box near the mother so she can see her brood, and keep them warm with a hot water bottle wrapped in a towel or an electric heating pad. When you have checked that each little fellow is perking normally, put him in the box. If whelping takes long, and the puppies are crying, you can give them one or two dropperfulls of warm milk—one cup water mixed with one teaspoon Karo is a good mixture.

But as soon as the mother is relaxed and labor is at an end, be sure to put the pups on her to nurse. The first milk of the mother, called *colustrum*, contains valuable vitamins and minerals and antibodies which give your puppy immunity to diseases while it is nursing. This first nursing also causes contractions in the uterus and helps expel any placental matter or even an unexpected puppy!

When the last puppy has arrived, your bitch is a new dog. She will be relaxed and easy. No more straining, no more anxiety. She will stretch out peacefully and count noses and then put her house to order. You can help by providing new papers and cleaning up.

It may seem impossible, with all that is going on, but you must try to keep count of the number of placentas which come out. There should be one for each puppy. Sometimes, the placenta comes with the puppy, sometimes it follows with the next. But if placenta matter is left inside the dog, it can be very dangerous and your veterinarian should be called. Many dogs eat the placenta, cord and sac. When dogs were wild and not domesticated, this may have served as extra food, but today it is just as well if you remove this material. You are interested in your dog's diet and won't let her starve, I'm sure!

Another thing breeders often advise is that you keep a record of the time of arrival of each puppy, his markings and weight, and any other characteristics.

Once in a great while a puppy is born with a deformity. This is very sad, and if the litter is small you will no doubt be quite upset. Harelip is one such congenital deformity, but today it is correctable by surgery. Oftentimes, with harelip, however, the puppy will also

After the puppies have been born, the dam should be taken to the veterinarian promptly. This is done so that she may be given a complete physical examination and injections to remove any placental matter that might still be in the uterus.

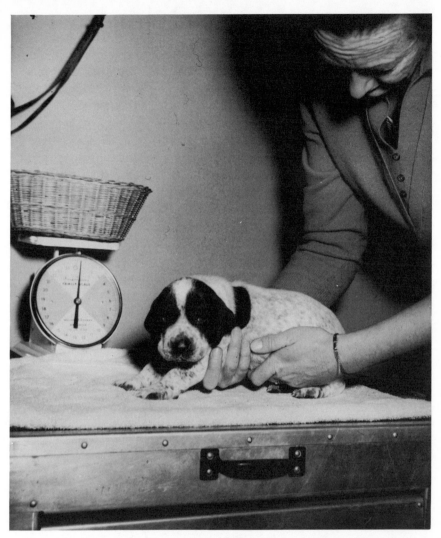

Most breeders keep weekly weight checks on their puppies. This gives an idea of the growth rate of the youngsters and is a barometer of their general well-being.

have a cleft palate. This prevents it from nursing properly and the dog will starve. Some puppies are born with other malformations, or perhaps the hind feet are turned as a result of the position in the uterus. Your veterinarian will tell you which of these conditions can be corrected and modern veterinary medicine has gone far in perfecting new surgical methods. Discuss your problems with your veterinarian and follow his instructions.

If you have no veterinarian in attendance be on the lookout for the following signs of trouble: labor lasting more than 4-6 hours with no success, excessive straining and pain, trembling and shivering with near exhaustion and collapse, vomiting. Puppies arriving feet first often mean more following in this manner with problems such as tangled and pinched umbilical cords. If any of these symptoms appear, call for help immediately.

We hope that these few problems have not discouraged you from breeding your bitch. Don't worry, most dogs have perfectly normal deliveries and your biggest problem will be to keep from taking the newborn pups away from their mother and cuddling them yourself. We mention problems mostly to help prepare you for any emergency which might arise when you have no professional help at hand.

FALSE PREGNANCY

Once in a great while, a bitch will show signs of pregnancy after being in heat, but will not be pregnant at all. Her abdomen will be swollen, the nipples red and puffy. These symptoms may disappear overnight or she may keep you in suspense until almost time to whelp. If you have any suspicions, consult your doctor. For one thing, if your dog was not impregnated, she may then be entitled to a return service, and your doctor should ascertain that there was no abortion or resorbing of the foetus. Also, false pregnancy is often a sign of illness or malfunctioning in the dog. Sometimes changes are caused by tumors, cysts or infections. If you want your next breeding to be successful, you will have to be sure that your bitch is healthy.

AFTERCARE

The aftercare of your bitch is one of general good health routines. You may have to feed her more often, but be careful not to let her get too fat. Be sure that the diet is properly balanced with lots of protein and milk. If she seems a little constipated (after all, her insides have been severely jolted) a little mineral oil will help.

There is one thing to look out for in your nursing mother. Dogs which produce large amounts of milk or have very large litters often develop a form of convulsion known as *eclampsia* or suckling fits. This seems to be caused by a calcium deficiency caused by loss to the mother during nursing. If this happens, she will start to stagger, lose coordination and suffer from convulsions and often fall unconscious. Call your veterinarian immediately. The most common cure is large doses of calcium given by injection. Plenty of protein after that can keep eclampsia from recurring.

Mastitis is another illness that can plague the dam. This is an infection of the breasts. It causes the milk to become extremely acid and this affects the puppies. It used to be thought that dam's milk had to be alkaline and that any acidity would be injurious to the puppies. This is untrue, as bitch's milk is either neutral or slightly acid naturally. Extreme acidity, however, like any extreme, is dangerous. Using limewater will not cure the condition. The mother dog must be seen by a veterinarian and medicated properly, as soon as possible. The puppies will have to be fed a substitute formula until she is cured, or else weaned altogether.

As for your newborn puppies, more in the next chapter, but there are one or two things to note. For the most part, puppies, like human babies, want to eat and sleep the first week. If they are unhappy about something, they cry.

If one of the puppies seems weaker than the others, put him on the rear nipples. These are bigger and he can get a better hold. You may even have to help him hang on if he has trouble. Another problem which occurs occasionally is when the mother fails to lick her puppy when he is newborn and stimulate elimination. This licking is the only way the puppy can be stimulated to urinate. If she doesn't do this, you are elected. But it's easy enough. Just rub the puppy's tummy and anus with a soft piece of cotton which is dampened with warm water and wait for the puddle. In a few days, he can manage it by himself and you will have plenty of puddles.

Chapter VII

Puppyhood

INTRODUCTION

Have you breathed a sigh of relief? Your dog has come through with flying colors; she has produced a lively, hungry, healthy litter of puppies. Not only that, she is taking care of them with all the love and vigilance a dog can command. Every single puppy is inspected each time it passes review in front of her; each is carefully washed and licked. And she provides her own built-in supply of milk, already bottled and warmed. When she leaves to eat or go outside for a breather, she rushes back afterwards and once again counts noses, just in case she lost one.

Indeed, the mother dog provides all that nature requires: food, warmth, cleanliness and love. When the puppies are old enough, she knows when to wean and how to wean them away from her.

Occasionally, however; problems arise and if so, your veterinarian can help you. Good medical advice and common sense care should prevent any mishaps.

THE NEST

In most cases, the whelping box also serves as the nursery until the puppies are old enough to sleep away from their mother. You may have to add to the sides as the puppies grow so they won't wander away. As long as you keep the papers changed and the box clean, there will be no problem. In addition, the doting mother helps keep the nest clean. She encourages the puppies to urinate and defecate and then cleans up the mess as well. After two or three weeks, however, she may stop, and then you become chambermaid. But take courage, it will soon be spring and then you can take the pups outdoors and your chores will become lighter.

Once in a while, if the mother is ill, or there are just too many

The period of puppyhood is a short one, and within that time a German Pointer will achieve his full, adult size. This rapid, early growth rate must be accompanied by the best in feeding and care if the individual is to mature to full potential.

demanding little fellows for her to handle, she may neglect to encourage elimination and cleanliness. If this occurs, you can help the puppies to urinate by rubbing their bottoms round and round just like the mother does with her tongue. If they are sore, rub a little vaseline in also. But you may have to clean up afterwards as well!!

If the mother, for some reason, is not in the nest to help warm the puppies, be sure to provide warmth. You can use an electric heating pad made just for this purpose. They are available at your petshop.

DIET

Most dams have an adequate supply of milk which lasts three to four weeks without supplementing. Occasionally, the litter may be

A great deal of time and effort goes into the proper raising of a well-bred litter, but in the long run it always proves worth the bother. If this were not true people would not stay in the sport of dogs at all.

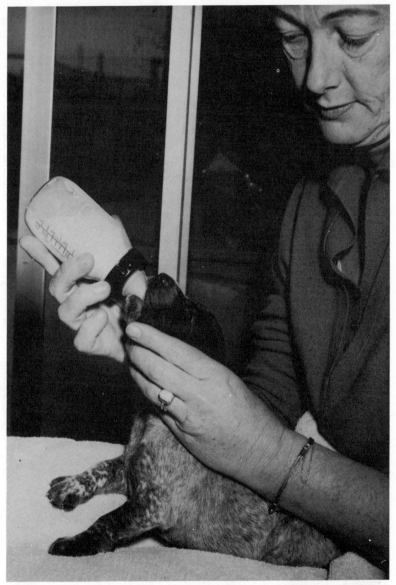

Hand-feeding a litter of puppies is a most arduous task, but it sometimes must be done if the young ones are to survive. Ordinary cow's milk is not a good formula by itself but if it is modified to more closely approach bitches' milk it can be used. The best alternative is any of the new simulated bitches' milks made for feeding very young puppies. Any good pet shop will have complete stocks available.

A German
Wirehaired
Pointer of the
Odin strain. This
is the type upon
which most of the
the American-
bred Wirehairs
have been
developed.

so large or the milk so scanty that you have to help out. A foster mother is ideal, but available foster mothers (and willing owners) are hard to find. If you are so fortunate, you will find that it is not hard to accustom the new mother to her new pups. Rub a little of her milk on the puppies' tummies and let her lick it off. In no time at all, they are friends, and if you leave them in a quiet, out-of-the-way place, they will soon be old friends.

But suppose you are not so lucky, and you find that *you* are the substitute mother. It's back to baby bottles and formula for you! If your dog's milk is scanty, you may only have to supplement several times a day, but if you are a full-time puppy mother, plan on at least five or six feedings per day. Surprisingly, the care of a young puppy is very similar to that of a young baby, except that puppies grow up faster and you quit walking the floor sooner.

It is most convenient to make up a large amount of formula in advance, refrigerate it, and then pour it into bottles and warm it to body temperature for each feeding. Be sure that the holes in the nipple are large enough and that, while feeding, you are careful that the puppy does not take in too much air (tilt the bottle so that the top and nipple are always full).

There are several excellent brands of simulated bitch's milk on the market. Follow directions, refrigerate and that's all there is. You may want to ask your veterinarian which brand he recommends.

The ideal homemade formula? There are as many as there are veterinarians. If you are making your own, however, remember that cow's milk contains less fat (4%) than bitch's milk (11%). Here are three typical formulas you can try:

(1)	(2)	(3)
1 oz. cream	6 oz. evaporated milk	2 oz. lactogen
1 oz. Nestle's Pelargon	3 oz. water	2 oz. cream (30% butterfat)
6 oz. water	$\frac{1}{2}$ tbs. corn syrup	4 oz. water

Refrigerate and warm when needed.

How much do you feed a young puppy? Most dog owners say until his tummy is full and he just lolls back, almost too full to move. You can also tell when he is finished as a little milk will bubble around his mouth. But this doesn't tell you how much formula to prepare. The following chart should help, but remember, these are typical amounts and if your puppies are obviously hungry, feed them some more. If the one you select agrees with the pups, don't change. A change in the diet of a young puppy can be disastrous.

This is a good point to remember if you are selling or giving puppies away when they have weaned. Give some of the same type of food you have been giving your puppies to the new owners, or include instructions, so that the puppy's diet does not change.

Amount of formula per feeding in ounces	Weight of puppy in pounds
1 oz.	$\frac{3}{4}$ lb.
1$\frac{3}{4}$ oz.	1 lb.
2 oz.	2 lbs.
2$\frac{3}{4}$ oz.	3 lbs.

If you are only supplementing, you won't have to make up too much, but if you are feeding the puppies completely, better make up a two days' supply at once. Unless the puppies are very tiny, you can probably start them on dish feeding quite soon. If you are having trouble getting a young puppy to drink out of a dish (and after all, what has a dish to offer, it just isn't mother) try dipping its lips into

Weanlings are often reluctant to leave their mothers' food supply, but once introduced to dish feeding they usually take to the new procedure quite readily.

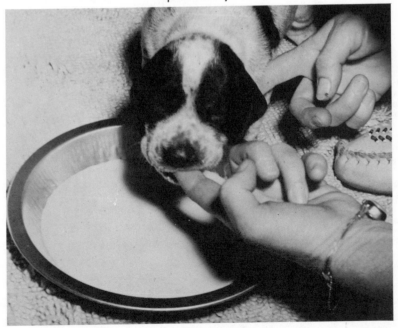

the dish. Instinct will cause him to lick it up and before you know it, that smart fellow will have his mug in the dish and be lapping it up.

The above formulae can also be used when weaning the puppies until you put them on whole milk.

WEANING

Puppies will usually nurse for three to four weeks and then gradually slacken, but you can start weaning them yourself as early as 15 to 16 days, using the proper foods. If left to wean without your help, your mother dog will appear to be doing a most unladylike act—she will regurgitate partially digested food for her pups to eat. She isn't sick; this is just instinctive with dogs. Wild dogs, having no prepared puppy meal or canned and packaged foods, used this as the first food for their helpless puppies, but you can start the puppies on supplementary foods and relieve your dog of this chore. By now your puppies are much livelier and their eyes are open. They are aware of the world—their mother and their box and those strange

Opinions vary on giving each puppy his own dish or letting the litter feed from the same pan. Some say communal feeding makes the puppies more keen. Others argue that individual dishes assure each puppy will get the same amount of food. In the end it is up to each individual owner to decide for himself.

Weanlings should be started on warmed, evaporated milk mixed with equal parts of water. From here they can be fed baby cereal or puppy meal and after they have learned to accept this they can be offered meat.

people who make cooing noises at them. They may even have tried a little exploring and fallen out of the box once or twice. They wobble a bit, it is true, but they are on their feet, almost.

All this activity and the activity to come mean that the foods you give your dogs now are important. There are excellent preparations on the market for your newly weaned puppy. Use any of the puppy meals; they contain all the necessary nutrients for a rapidly growing pup. Many breeders feel that Pablum or baby cereals are not nutritious enough for such explosive growth, but people do use them with no apparent ill effects. If you use puppy meal or any cereal food, be sure to add milk and fat.

One way of getting a puppy to take to his new diet is to put a little on your finger and let him lick it off. Before you know it, he'll be licking the platter clean. Some people also add scraped beef to a puppy's diet. This is a bother to make, but you may feel it is necessary. Using a spoon or the back of a knife, scrape along the piece of beef (bottom round is fine) so that what you get is almost liquid beef, beef minus the gristle and connective tissue. Vitamins and mineral supplements are also recommended.

We like to see each puppy with his own dish. This is because the runts (there are often some in the litter) sometimes get pushed aside by the bigger pups; this method gives every puppy his share. Be sure also to have a water dish with fresh water available.

Here is a typical feeding schedule for your weaned puppy.

Age	7 a.m.	Noon	5 p.m.	10 p.m.
4 to 12 weeks	x	x	x	x
3 to 6 months	x	x	x	
6 to 12 months	x		x	
1 year and on			x	

Gradually increase the amount of food you give the dog if he needs it. An active dog requires more food than a dog that is penned up most of the time.

PUPPY DIET

Pointer puppies need lots of bone-building foods—meat, milk and fat. The following amounts of food are recommended for your Shorthair or Wirehair. Of course, you can add or subtract according to his appetite. No dog should be forced to eat more than he wants or allowed to go very hungry.

Age	7 a.m.	Noon	5 p.m.	10 p.m.
Weaning to 3 months	½ cup baby cereal or dog meal, water or milk	½ cup warm milk with cereal or biscuits	2 tbs. chopped beef, 2 tbs. cereal or meal, vitamins and mineral supplement	½ cup warm milk with ¼ cup cereal

Baby cereal or puppy meal may be used. Gradually switch to dog meal.

Age	7 a.m.	Noon	5 p.m.	10 p.m.
3 to 6 months	½ cup meat with cereal or meal	1 cup milk, soft boiled egg 2 times a week or 1 cup cottage cheese	½ cup meat with ½ cup dog meal or kibble and water. Vitamin and mineral supplement	
6 to 12 months	½ cup dog meal with cottage cheese or egg and milk. Vitamin and mineral supplement		½ cup meat with ¾ cup kibble or meal, fat, scraps	

Be sure to include fat for a shiny, healthy coat.

Before he goes on a diet of solid food the young puppy may be given liquid vitamins from a dropper. It is best to consult your veterinarian and follow his advice on the subject.

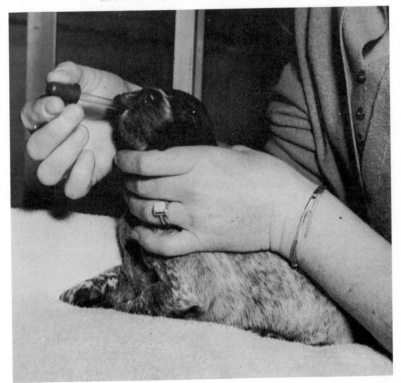

SPECIAL CHARACTERISTICS OF THE GERMAN POINTER PUPPY

Docking the tail: German Shorthairs and Wirehairs have their tails docked to about 2/5 their original length. This can be done by the veterinarian by the fourth day after birth. If you are forced to do it yourself, docking is not too difficult, and it is relatively painless for the puppy. Using a sterile scissors, pull the skin of the tail back and then cut the tail at the first or second joint. Then pull the skin forward, and it will form a flap which heals over the cut. We suggest that the sterile quarters of the veterinarian are best for this operation. It also affords him time to examine each puppy.

DEWCLAWS

Dewclaws are small vestigial claws found on the forelegs of some breeds. If your dog is born with dewclaws it is best to trim them off. Because the nails are not worn down as are the other nails on a dog's feet, they can become ingrown and cause infection. Dewclaws can be cut off by the third or fourth day.

WORMING

Chapter XII describes parasites and how they infect dogs. You may be surprised to learn, however, that very young puppies can be infested with parasites, which they pick up from their mother's body, possibly even before they are born. Three-week-old puppies can be wormed with no harmful results. Some breeders worm their litters as a matter of course and don't wait until the parasites put in an appearance. By then it is often too late. Consult with your veterinarian about dosages or let him do it if you are nervous. When worming is done, be sure that your puppies are in good health, or any dose, no matter how safe it is ordinarily, will be harmful. Follow the veterinarian's advice exactly.

TEETH

Puppies, like human babies, are not born with teeth, although there are always exceptions. And like humans, they have two sets of teeth, first or baby teeth and second teeth. The first baby teeth to

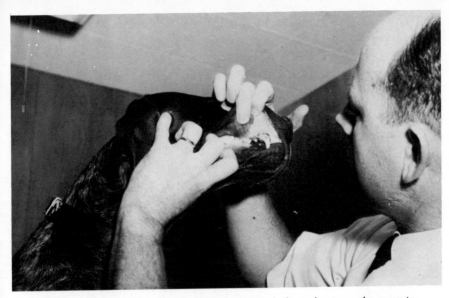

The dog's mouth contains 42 permanent teeth. In order to make certain these will be as strong as possible it is necessary to give the puppy a well-balanced diet and to make sure that when the second teeth erupt, the milk teeth are not still in his mouth. This may cause, crooked, incorrect dentition.

erupt are the incisors (front teeth). These push out by about 4-5 weeks, and after them come the canines (these are like our eye teeth). The incisors fall out at about 4-5 months and the canines a month or so later. The molars arrive at 5 months, 6 and 7 months. A dog has a full complement of 42 teeth, 20 in the lower jaw and 22 in the upper.

When the teeth are erupting, if the puppy has any illness the enamel will not be deposited on the teeth or the teeth may be pitted or discolored. If the first teeth have not fallen out and the second are arriving, you may have to have the first teeth pulled so that the others will come in straight.

Veterinarians advise that you have your dog's teeth cleaned regularly, as tartar often coats them heavily and then it is difficult to remove.

HERNIA

As your puppy grows, you may see a small lump over the navel.

This means that the navel has failed to heal properly and the bulge is a hernia. If the deformity is slight, there is no danger, but if the opening in the abdomen is large enough, a loop of intestine can work out into the sac. You will have to have your veterinarian repair the hernia or strangulation might occur.

VACCINATIONS

Veterinary medicine has experimented for many years to find vaccines for several of the more severe diseases of dogdom. The following chart is a recommended schedule for vaccinations. See your veterinarian for inoculations. There are newer and better vaccines being prepared all the time, and your puppy's life may be saved by one of these recent discoveries.

INOCULATION TIME TABLE FOR DOGS

6 weeks*	8 weeks	10 weeks	3 months	5-6 months
(1) Hepatitis Anti-Serum (protection)	Distemper, Hepatitis and Leptospirosis Vaccine (3 in 1)	Distemper, Hepatitis and Leptospirosis Vaccine (3 in 1)	Canine Distemper Vaccine	Rabies Vaccine**
(2) Anti-Canine Distemper Homologous Serum (protection)				

REGISTRATION PAPERS

There are two steps in registering a purebred dog with the American Kennel Club. First the owner of the litter must send in a litter application with all the details properly filled in. This is sent to the American Kennel Club. When the dog is purchased, the new owner can apply for an individual certificate, with the dog's name and pedigree. Some breeders have already done this, so that all the new owner must do is have the registration papers transferred to his name.

---

*During the nursing period, puppies are immune to distemper. Protective serum is given immediately after weaning, until permanent vaccination can take place. Recent experimentation at Cornell University has shown that most dogs acquire immunity from their mothers. It is important that permanent vaccination take place after this immunity has worn off. Distemper vaccine should also be administered yearly.
**Rabies shots should be given once a year.

The purchaser of a puppy should receive a registration certificate, or application, a three-generation pedigree and a health certificate. The registration certificate, or application, should be sent together with a stated fee to the American Kennel Club, 51 Madison Avenue New York City, for registration in the new owner's name.

COMMON DISEASES OF PUPPYHOOD

In Chapter XII diseases are discussed in detail, so this section includes only a few of the common diseases. Be sure to consult the vaccination chart also, as prevention is far more effective than any cure.

Infected Navel: In a small puppy watch out for an infected navel. This is often caused by rough or hard surfaces in the nest. The navel is rubbed and becomes infected. The veterinarian will have to clean it and medicate. The best prevention is to provide a soft bed for your puppies.

Distemper: Distemper is a disease which infects many puppies. It is often fatal or it leaves the puppy with nervous ailments or other serious after effects. Until a puppy is weaned, he is safe, but after that, you must protect him with vaccine. If your puppy becomes feverish, his nose and eyes runny, and his stomach upset, consult

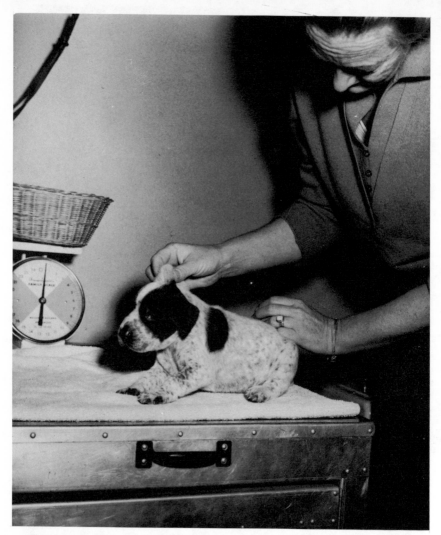

The period of weekly weight check is a good time to check the puppy over as to its general well-being. It is easier to take care of any problems when they are in the early stages than when they establish a foothold in the young animal.

your veterinarian immediately. The health of the whole litter is at stake.

Hard Pad: This ailment is most infectious to young puppies. They run a high fever with intestinal upsets. The foot pads are very tender. Call your veterinarian for treatment.

Parasites: We have already mentioned worming, but you can still keep an eye out for parasites such as fleas and ticks. They can infect a puppy at any age. If you keep the nest and other sleeping areas clean, there is less danger.

Deficiency Diseases: To prevent problems such as rickets or other deficiency diseases, be sure that your puppy's food is nourishing and well balanced. Remember that he is growing rapidly and needs more protein in the form of milk and meat, and more fat and vitamins than his elders.

Eye Infections: Once in a while, a tiny puppy's eyes become infected even before they open. The corner of the eye can be lifted up, the eye drained and medicated. See your veterinarian.

Diarrhea: When a puppy has diarrhea it is viewed as a serious condition. It may be caused by a change in the diet, spoiled food, or may be a symptom of a more serious illness. Your veterinarian should be contacted at once.

Chapter VIII

Diet

THE DIET IN GENERAL

Are you being watched by soulful eyes? Is every bite you eat at dinner followed by your dog, standing there licking his chops, as you put away a steak? And do you give in and slip him just a little bit, or a bone to gnaw on? DON'T, if you want your dog to be healthy as well as polite.

A well-fed, well-trained dog eats, at *his* dinner hour, only what you put in *his* dish. Encouraging dogs to eat food at other times only makes them dinner pests. It may also harm them nutritionally. Bad habits at the dinner table can lead a dog to beg from other people and this is even more dangerous. You know what's in your dinner plate, but unless the ladies have been exchanging recipes over the back fence, you may not know what your neighbor is feeding your dog.

There is, of course, the possibility that you have not been feeding your dog properly and that he is genuinely hungry. Whether he is hungry or just badly trained is for you to discover, but if it is malnutrition, symptoms will appear sooner or later. Surely it is wiser to check your pet's diet and see that it is made up of the essentials every dog needs.

When dogs were not yet domesticated, they ate what they killed, muscle, meat, innards, skin, bones, even the fur or hair. But we don't allow our dogs to forage for their own food any more (nor is there wild game available except in distant wooded areas) and we are responsible for giving them a proper meal. We must replace the ingredients which nature intended them to eat and which were found in the wild game they ate.

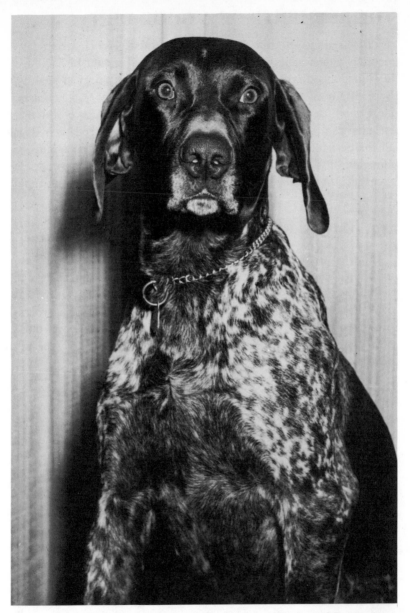

Both the German Shorthaired and the German Wirehaired Pointers are large powerful animals. They must have a good, highly nourishing diet and cannot be maintained in good condition on table scraps.

THE ELEMENTS OF A GOOD DIET

The essentials of your dog's diet are protein, carbohydrate, fats, vitamins and minerals. Each of these elements should be included in your dog's diet if he is to grow properly, look and feel healthy. Lack of any of the five essentials can cause a number of diseases, most of which are discussed in Chapter XII. Too much of any diet essential can also be harmful, however. People who feed their dogs all the best foods and then give them an extra dose of vitamins or minerals "just for good measure" may cause a toxic reaction in their pets. *Everything good in moderation* is a good motto for a proper diet.

PROTEINS

Proteins are found in meat, fish, some vegetables (such as soy bean) milk and cheese. They are used for essential body building. Meat can be fed your pet if it is fresh, dried or frozen (and thawed). If meat is dried, be sure that it is labeled "Vacuum Packed" as this process preserves the vitamins. Twenty to thirty percent of your dog's meal should be protein. If your dog is pregnant or nursing, she will need extra protein, and so do rapidly growing puppies.

CARBOHYDRATES

Carbohydrates should make up between 50 and 70% of your pet's dinner. They are found in cereals, vegetables, sugar, syrup and honey. Carbohydrates give a dog his boundless energy and help him grow. When starches are baked, the starches are converted into dextrin which tastes sweet. Most dogs have a sweet tooth and enjoy something sweet and tasty. But if you feed your dog too much carbohydrate, his diet will suffer, as he will eat less protein.

FATS

Fats are also important in a dog's daily ration. Bitch's milk naturally has more fat content than cow's milk, but once a dog is on adult food, he can drink regular milk, and not the enriched formula you fed him as a puppy. You must then add fat to his meal in other ways. This element is important as a vitamin reserve and as an aid for digestion by slowing the passage of food through the animal's

The show dog and the dog that is worked afield both need a more nourishing diet, higher in calories, than the average housepet. The owner must discover the proper amount and balance of food to keep his dog in good health and in optimum condition.

intestine. It also keeps his coat healthy and shiny. Fat provides $2\frac{1}{4}$ times as much energy as an equivalent amount of carbohydrate or protein, but you cannot give a dog too much fat, as this may cause diarrhea. Naturally a dog which uses up a tremendous amount of energy, such as a hunting dog, can use more, but for most family dogs too much fat will lead to trouble. Your dog's diet should have about 5% fat content (and not more than 25%) to be nourishing. Important sources of fats are butter, suet, lard, bacon fat and even vegetable shortening. An excellent and cheap fat is bacon fat or grease from your cooking. Fatty meat is far better than lean cuts, so do not think you are being kind if you buy only the best quality top round steak for your dog; he'll probably look underfed and his coat and skin will suffer.

VITAMINS

Vitamins are those elusive substances without which we would all be undernourished and diseased. They were first discovered by Casimir Funk, a Polish scientist, in 1911. You must see that your dog has a certain amount of vitamins, but remember that if you are feeding your dog a good diet, he will probably get all the vitamins he needs. Pregnant and nursing mothers and pups need supplements, however.

MINERALS

Minerals are also found in many foods and need not be supplemented unless there is a specific need for more. Minerals such as

A dog's general well-being is determined by many factors. One is his eagerness to dive into the food pan. These puppies leave little doubt as to their attitude toward mealtimes.

calcium and phosphorus are used to build bones and teeth and are found in milk, vegetables, eggs, soy beans, bone marrow, blood, liver and some cereals (whole grained).

Following is a table of vitamins and minerals, their use in the body and where they are found.

VITAMINS

A (and carotene)	*Use*	*Found in*
Stable at boiling temperatures	General living and growth	Alfalfa-leaf meal
	Skin health	Butter, carrots
Spoiled if exposed to air	Fertility, Hearing,	Egg yolks, carotene
	Digestion, Vision,	Fish liver, oil
Stored in body	Nerve health,	Glandular organs
Fat soluble	Prevention of infection	Leaves of plants
	Muscle coordination	Many dark green
	Pituitary gland function	vegetables

B Complex		
Biotin, Pantothenic Acid	Growth, Appetite, Ferti-	Yeast, cereals
Riboflavin, Thiamine	lity, Nerve and Heart	Eggs, milk, liver,
Folic Acid, Niacin	health, Liver and gastro-	alfalfa meal
Pyrodoxin	intestinal function	Rapidly growing
Water soluble, some destroyed by high heat	Lactation, Intestinal absorption	plants
		Bacterial growth
Biotin negated by raw egg whites	Muscle function, Blood health, Bladder and kidney function	Cattle paunch and intestinal contents
	Prevention of anemia, black tongue and Vincent's disease	

D		
Irradiated ergosterol	Regulates calcium and	Fish liver and oil
Stored by body and can stand heat	phosphorus in blood	Some animal fats
	Regulates Metabolism	
Resists decomposition	Normal skeletal develop-	
Fat soluble	ment and muscular coordination	
	Lactation	
	Prevents rickets	

E		
Tocopherol	Survival of young puppies	Seed germ and
Stored in body		germ oils
Spoils if exposed to air		
Stand ordinary cooking temperatures		
Fat Soluble		

F		
Unsaturated fatty acids	Coat and skin health	Wheat germ oil
		Linseed oil
		Other seed oils

K
Fat soluble Antidote for Warfarin rat poison	Blood clotting	Alfalfa-leaf meal

MINERALS:
Calcium
90% stored in bones	Bones, teeth, blood component Lactation, Fertility Muscle, nerve, heart function	Bones and bone meal Milk Alfalfa-leaf meal

Phosphorus
Stored in bones, blood, muscles and teeth	Bones, teeth Carbohydrate and Fat metabolism Blood component Liquid content of tissues	Cereals, milk Fish, bones, meat (generally abun- dant in dogs diet)

Iron
Need in minute amounts Stored in body—65% in blood; 30% in liver, marrow, spleen; 5% in muscle tissue	Red blood cells Transports oxygen in blood Prevents anemia	Egg yolk, liver Innards, bone marrow Meat

Potassium
	Body fluid regulator Blood regulator Muscle function	Blood Vegetables, potatoes

Sodium
Found in body with phosphorus, chlorine and sulphur	Regulates body fluids, blood Component of gastric juices and urine	Table salt Blood

Chlorine
	Same as above	

Iodine
Found in thyroid gland	Thyroid health, meta- bolism	Foods grown in iodine-rich soil Fish meal from salt water fish

Magnesium
Needed in tiny amounts	Muscles, bones Nerve and blood function Growth	Bones, vegetables

Copper
Needed in tiny amounts	Forms hemoglobin with iron	Blood, copper sulphate

Sulphur
Needed in tiny but regular amounts	Body regulation	Meat, egg yolks

CALORIES

Calories are not ingredients of food, but the unit used to measure heat—and food when it is eaten, digested and used can be measured in terms of calories. We are all of us very conscious of weight nowadays. We must not only watch our own figures but our dog's as well. Dogs can eat 30 to 50 percent more food than they need and still be hungry. Very small dogs, between 5 and 10 pounds, need 250 to 600 calories daily. Dogs weighing between 15 and 25 pounds use at least 600 to 1,000 calories and dogs from 30 to 60 pounds use up 1,100 to 2,000 calories. If your dog is eating more than he should, you may have to put him on a diet, or hope for a dog-type food substitute. Check the caloric value of the food you serve your dog.

COMMON TYPES OF DIETS

You now know the elements of a proper diet for your dog, but you

There are many kinds of foods and feeding methods available to dog owners. The feeding program will determine whether a young, well-bred puppy like the two shown here will mature into the full flower of their genetic inheritance.

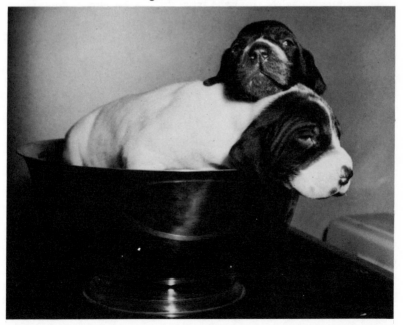

may be wondering how to apply all this knowledge to what to put into your dog's dinner plate. There are a number of different types of diets available. Your pocketbook and the type of household you have will determine what kind of food you feed your dog. Your dog's size will dictate how much food you must provide. Certain types of hounds are deliberately kept thin, but most dogs look and feel best when their bodies are filled out, their coats glossy and the skin healthy. This is achieved with a proper diet. Remember that puppies will eat much more than adult dogs in terms of their weight, and that active dogs will consume more than their less active canine brothers.

TABLE SCRAPS—OR HOME DIETS

Nowadays, with modern methods of refrigeration and freezing, there is very little left over after meal times. Most food is consumed, and the scraps often used by the thrifty housewife to concoct the latest casserole the next day. Thus, it would appear that in order to feed your dog properly from table scraps, you have to purchase more food than you eat. Spoiled food, of course, is for the garbage can, not the feeding dish. The only leftover that you can give him easily and cheaply is surplus grease and gravies. But if you do choose to feed your dog solely from the table, he can eat almost anything. Just be sure that all the ingredients listed in the food essentials are included, with plenty of protein. Fried foods and cakes and cookies are not recommended.

A homemade dinner for your pet can be made up as follows: ground fatty beef or liver, innards or even cottage cheese to provide protein, some green or yellow vegetables, a cereal such as oatmeal or day-old whole wheat bread spread with butter and crumbled up, milk or warm water, a cooked egg several times a week, even cooked fruit, and of course leftover gravies, fat and scraps. Of course, this can cost you from 50c. to $3 per day per dog!

CANNED DOG FOOD

Canned dog food is very cheap and very easy to prepare—a can opener is all you need. But be sure if you use this as the staple diet of your dog, that you know the true cost of the food and the protein content. Most canned dog food contains 70-75% water and the remaining 25% is food. A good-sized dog will need at least 2-3 cans of dog food a day, if it is not supplemented with other foods, regardless of what the label tells you. Another thing to watch out for is the quality of the canned food, although this may be difficult to discover. It is sad, but true, that many canned dog foods are not high quality and that the meat is of such low quality that you would never knowingly feed it to your pet. There are some good quality products, of course, put up by companies genuinely concerned with your dog's health and well being. Compare the protein and fat guarantees printed on the label. The more of each, the better the food. Or ask your veterinarian to recommend a good canned dog food and check the label for content. The Dept. of Agriculture issues a seal of approval for canned dog food which meets minimum nutritional standards.

KIBBLES WITH MEAT AND VEGETABLES

Kibbles are a form of biscuit but they are by no means a complete diet. Flour is the chief ingredient and as it is baked it is converted into dextrin which tastes sugary. Dogs love it and lick their lips for more. But the baking process destroys the vitamin and mineral content while it increases its dog appeal. Therefore you must add meat, vegetables and, often, vitamin and mineral supplements. You may find it is a nuisance to mix. If kibbles are used with no other added foods, this menu can cause serious diet deficiency diseases and even convulsions.

PELLETS

A number of commercial dried dog foods are available in pellet form. They can be eaten dry or with a little water, and extra water served on the side. Their chief attraction seems to be that they are easy to pour and "look nice."

MEALS (OR DRY DOG FOOD)

By far the most popular food in kennels is dog meal. It is also the most versatile of the packaged dog foods. All the essential vitamins and minerals are added in sufficient quantities, as well as protein. Some brands carry as much as 30% protein. If you use 1½ ounces of fat to 5 ounces of high quality meal, you have a dinner that cannot be surpassed for quality, nourishment and dog satisfaction. As an added inducement, it is easy to prepare, and extremely economical. Pregnant and nursing mothers will need extra milk and meat with their regular dinner. Special puppy meals are also available for growing dogs.

EXTRUDED FOODS

Extruded foods are a fairly new product made in the same way as puffed wheat or rice. The granules of starch are heated under great pressure and when the pressure is suddenly released, the granules explode—they are shot from guns as the ads say! Of course, this food tastes sweet and is enthusiastically greeted by dogs and you may think that this is an ideal food. But this eagerness may be hunger—real hunger. The food is blown up to twice its original size, and therefore the animal eats only one half his usual ration and he is full. But he is only getting one half his needs. The results are hunger and undernourishment, surely a poor investment for your pet.

DIET COST

Following is a table showing the various diets and their relative cost, based on feeding a 25-pound dog 900 calories a day. The prices may vary somewhat, depending on where you live.

	Type of Diet	Cost per day	Cost per year
1.	Table scraps	$ .50	$182.50
2.	Canned dog food (2 for 29c.)	.29	105.85
3.	Kibbles, meat, vegetables, supplement vitamins—18c. per lb., others app. vitamin supp. 5c. per day)	.38	138.00
4.	Pellets 15c. per pound	.084	30.66
5.	Dry dog food plus fat (14c. per pound for meal, fat free from your table)	.04	15.70

The above list shows that the last type of diet is by far the most economical. The authors suggest that when you are planning your first trip to the market or pet store for supplies for your new pet, that you take this book along or a list of the necessary elements for a good diet. Check the contents of each type of dog food and the cost.

Once you find a good nutritious diet for your dog, stick to it, as changes can cause intestinal upsets, especially in puppies. Of course, if your dog is hardy and has a good digestion, you may find yourself adding leftovers to his basic diet, especially those he loves. But be sure that these tidbits do not take the place of the really important proteins, vitamins and minerals. For a treat, you can give your dog biscuits or dog yummies. A friend with a large, active, almost grown dog finds that biscuits are a fine substitute for furniture. Whenever she finds that her dog is about to test the durability of the sofa, she gives him a handful of dog treats and this satisfies him.

QUANTITY

Just how much do you give a dog? Breeders recommend that you plan on ½ to 1 ounce of food per pound of body weight, depending on the amount of exercise and the age of the dog. Feed your dog once or, in winter, twice a day. Oftentimes, in winter, dogs appreciate a light breakfast in order to help them face the school bus, mailman, garbage man and other sundry daytime activities. The main meal, however, should be given in late afternoon or early evening.

WATER

Have water available at all times. If you do not wish to keep the water dish out, offer water at least three times a day. You may want to restrict water to a puppy just before night, or in the case of illness.

DISHES

The best type of dishes are aluminum, but you can also purchase plastic or ceramic feeding pans. They do not chip or break easily, and can be cleaned quickly. Be sure that feeding and water pans are clean at all times. When you set out your dog's dinner, allow him at least 20-30 minutes to eat it, but then take it away and do not feed your dog until his next regularly scheduled meal time. This keeps him from being finicky and picky about his food. Naturally, if he is ill or has some diet problems, you will have to adjust. Another hint is to be sure that the food is not too sloppy and watery, so it's not messy.

Put your dog's dish in the same place at every feeding, preferably a spot where he won't be disturbed.

A TYPICAL DIET

Pointers of one year and over are large, active dogs. They need plenty of food to give them energy. If you use your dog for hunting,

A good diet need not be complicated to be beneficial, but sometimes dietary modifications must be introduced to fit the specific needs of a given animal.

you will find that he needs extra amounts of protein and fat. Feed your dog twice a day if necessary. For a normal-sized dog plan on about 4 cups meal with 1 lb. of meat. You can use water or milk to moisten the meal; add a coddled egg occasionally and, of course, fat or grease.

SPECIAL FEEDING PROBLEMS

Pregnant Bitches: Pregnant bitches need extra food, especially meat and milk, as well as extra vitamins. Feed your dog as much as she wants, but make sure that she doesn't get overweight. Toward the end of her pregnancy, keep the meals light.

Nursing mothers: Lactating bitches also need extra food, with meat, milk and vitamins especially essential. You may find it better to give her several meals a day so her milk will be rich.

Weaning: The chapter on puppyhood (Chapter VII) discusses puppy diet. The main thing to remember is that bitch's milk is richer than cow's milk and that when the puppies are weaned, you will have to add fat to the milk you feed them. You must also plan that puppies eat much more than adult dogs of the same size. Once they grow up their food intake will stabilize, but while they are growing, be sure to feed them highly nutritious foods and rich milk. There are several excellent puppy foods which can be mixed with milk and used for puppies.

Reducing: Overweight is a national concern. Everyone is on a diet, it seems, and diet foods and fads are a billion dollar business in this country. Your dog may not be conscious of his or her figure, but you should be aware of it. Fat dogs are prone to illness and unfit for showing. But dieting is heartrending. After all your dog doesn't know what it is all about and he can't rejoice in every lost pound on the scale. You MUST resist his appeals for more food, and tell your children (sternly) not to feed him, also.

To help a dog reduce, cut his caloric intake down so that he must live on his stored fat. If your dog normally eats 900 calories, then cut him down to 500. One cup of dog meal plus water should be enough. In ten days he will have lost about 1 pound. Exercise is also helpful. Check with your veterinarian for a proper diet for your pet if he is overweight.

Chapter IX

Training

PRINCIPLES OF TRAINING

In today's world of fast-moving cars and crowded cities and suburbs, the life of a dog is truly a *dog's life* if he is improperly trained. The many hazards of living mean the survival of the fittest—and to be fit for today's world a dog must be properly trained to obey his master (or mistress).

The methods are standard with dog trainers—positive training which relies on encouragement and reward, either by praise from the trainer or food, and negative training where mistakes are punished. Combinations of these methods are common.

With either reward or punishment, animal training requires that each step be taught slowly and completely before the next step is introduced. Rewards (positive training) can be *praise* by tone of voice and petting, or *food* such as a favorite tidbit, dog candy or biscuits. Dogs trained negatively with punishment—and some trainers advocate switches or chains thrown near the dogs, paper, or hitting—may become vicious. By and large, most dogs respond to violence in kind. Dogs are not born vicious; they are made so. The uncontrollable dog could have been saved by thoughtful training work when he was young or less wild. Sadly, in most cases, the dog who is mean or wild has to be destroyed, or is killed as a result of his foolhardy actions.

There are two types of training your dog can have—*general training* which makes it possible for him to live with the family in peace, and *specialized training* to qualify for the AKC Obedience Trials. Of course, you can also teach your dogs many tricks such as

True to their Germanic heritage both the Shorthair and the Wirehair have shown themselves to be highly intelligent and most amenable to training. They have excelled not only as gun dogs but as obedience performers and in most other areas where the dog is called upon to serve the needs of man.

Any trainer must expect to encounter puppy playfulness in working with a young animal. The way to get around this is to let the pupil grow with his education. Never should a dog with good temperament be trained in a manner that will break his spirit.

playing dead or begging, for your own enjoyment. Hunting dogs, police and army dogs, and other working breeds need special training.

It is most often taught by experts in the field rather than by lay persons.

When you begin training remember the following: your puppy is anxious to obey you, and is really trying hard even if he doesn't quite succeed at first. Every ounce of puppy love wants to please you. If he can't quite make it the first time, be PATIENT. He will make the grade in time when his muscles are all working properly and he has mastered the first steps. Be CONSISTENT. Use the same word for the same command, and react the same way to his success or lack of success. Don't laugh at something he does one time and then punish him for it the next. Use your VOICE, not your hand, to punish. Very little can be accomplished by beating a dog except to frighten him.

Teach your dog ONE STEP AT A TIME. He can't learn the more complicated actions until he has mastered the elementary ones. REWARD your dog immediately if he does it right. Although you can use a treat, we believe that by complimenting your dog and showing him with your voice and mannerisms what a wonderful dog he is, how marvelously well he has learned to sit and how pleased everyone is with him, that he will answer with the determination and willingness to learn more. PUNISH your dog if he refuses or disregards your commands by speaking angrily to him and making him realize that you are displeased; do not use violence or withhold basic necessities such as food.

HOUSEBREAKING

Do you have a new puppy? Or has one of the litter remained behind? The very first training you will have to start is *housebreaking*. This is imperative if everyone is to live together harmoniously and in clean quarters. But puppies, like children, cannot be completely trained until they are more mature physically. When you hear of a toilet trained child of nine months, you can be sure that his mother is trained, not the baby. And so it is with dogs. Most dogs cannot be completely and reliably housebroken until four months of age, when their bladder and anus are under control. This is no cause for despair, however; there is plenty you can do until then to keep the house and your dog's quarters clean.

Most dogs are first paper-broken, unless they live outdoors. A dog will not deliberately mess his bed, but he will look around for a

Paper training is a convenience for many dog owners while a puppy is being inoculated or before he is broken to the lead. Although most German Pointers, by reason of their size, are not paper trained an owner might, for his own reasons, want a puppy to use paper.

convenient corner. The first thing you must do with a young puppy is to confine him to a fairly small space and cover that space with newspaper. Then he can mess to his heart's content.

If you allow your puppy freedom of the house, you are asking for trouble. But if he does get out and make a puddle right in the middle of the floor, be sure to wipe it up thoroughly. Use a special dog scent to remove the odor, or your dog will make a beeline for that spot the minute he escapes again. Once he is trained, you can gradually allow him the run of the house, but keep an eye on him for danger signs.

Dogs instinctively use the same place over and over again. Observe which corner he calls his own, and gradually begin removing the paper until only that spot is covered. Leave a bit of soiled paper there so that the odor will attract him back. Praise him lavishly if he continues to use the spot. Be sure he knows that you are terribly pleased that he has been such a good dog. Of course, he probably won't know what it's all about for a while, but that's all right; he

Housebreaking is often facilitated by having a puppy sleep in a crate throughout the night. Dogs are naturally clean animals and take an aversion to soiling their beds. Crating encourages control in the young animal.

loves it anyway. Dog scents are available at most petshops to aid you in training your dog should you prefer a more sanitary training method.

As your dog grows up a bit, you will notice that he has to eliminate less and less. Mostly he goes right after naps, meals or play. Now is the time to start housebreaking. Those people who live in apartments have a more difficult job. They must note the signs, pick up the dog, rush to the elevator and race outside to the nearest curb, trying to attach the leash and desperately hoping the dog won't wet in some embarrassing place like the elevator. If you live in a house or garden apartment, your job is considerably easier. As soon as you observe the dog beginning to sniff around or go in circles, grab him and head for the outdoors. Be sure to praise and pat him generously when he cooperates. If you lead him to the same spot each day, the odor will remind him of his job. It's amazing how quickly your dog will learn what all these mad dashes outside mean and obey you willingly. Besides, he generally has to go! This does make it easier. There will

While he is being housebroken, the young Pointer's water supply should be under some control. It is unwise to allow such puppies to drink too near their bedtimes.

be lapses occasionally. If your dog wets the rug or messes the kitchen floor, immediately chastise him with your voice. Let him know how ashamed you are and how disgusted you feel. Never hit him, never rub his nose in his own mess, and never wait an hour or so before punishment. Dogs have short memories when they are young, and even 15 minutes later he won't have the least idea what you are talking about. If the lapse is just temporary, you are in luck. Occasionally you may have to begin again. This sounds discouraging, but it is the only way to housebreak him properly.

The following hints may be helpful:

1. **Remember that your small puppy has to go quite frequently, and you should be prepared to take him out. You must plan to be home while this basic training is completed.**
2. **Remember to take him out after naps, meals, play, or any excitement (such as strangers in the house or other dogs).**
3. **Praise your dog when he cooperates. Use your voice only when he forgets. And don't expect him to learn the day you begin. Training takes time and the dog must be physically mature.**
4. **If you let your puppy roam the house, you are asking for trouble; keep him confined to one room until you are absolutely sure.**

EARLY TRAINING

COME: This should be the first actual training you give your dog aside from housebreaking, and it is the most important. Once your dog learns to **come** when you call, he is safe from many dangers, and more easily handled.

A puppy should not be forced, so the easiest way to begin training him to **come** is to begin while is he in the house. Just coax him to you, saying **come** in your most wheedling voice. If there is no other big attraction—such as dinner or strangers—who should he come to but you, who else is so willing to play and means warm food and affection? He will sidle up at the sound of your voice, just begging for a pat. And of course you give him one. Repeat this several times a day, using only the one word **come**. Do not keep the lesson up for long and don't punish if he does not obey. Try again, perhaps with a bit of food. When he obeys fairly well, try it outside. Select a quiet

Teaching a dog to come when called is an essential part of his education and of great importance to his safety. He should be taught this on lead first and off lead when he is reliable.

spot and call **come**. If he refuses to come to you, take courage in hand and run off. You may fear you will lose him but no puppy can refuse a good chase with his master. If you look around you will see him manfully trying to catch up with you. When he does come up, praise him, pet him, make a big fuss, don't scold him for not obeying immediately.

Once your dog has begun to catch on to the new word in his vocabulary, you can begin adding his name, so he gets used to that. **Come, Kippy** and then **Kippy, come** will teach him his rightful name.

NO and **STOP:** About the same time as you begin teaching your puppy to come to you, you will probably find yourself telling him **no** or **stop.** He's in and out of mischief, and you are spending your days trailing him around to see that he isn't puddling as well as keeping him from chewing up the furniture and turning over the garbage can. If he does get into something he shouldn't, shout a loud **no** or **stop** and then take him away firmly. If he's bent on chewing, give him a rawhide bone and confine him to his room. But be sure and practice consistency. What is forbidden one time should also be forbidden the next, or you may find yourself with a very confused puppy. As a rule it isn't enough just to say **no,** but you must also remove him from the temptation or take the temptation away from him.

Stop can be used when you want the puppy to stop some activity such as biting, barking and growling. Often you will have to close his mouth and hold it shut while you chastise him with **stop** and a most sorrowful look.

LEAD TRAINING

Your dog is housebroken and almost knows when to **come,** and you can begin to think about lead (leash) training. Again, you must have time for training. If you have no spare time, perhaps it would be

Lead training a puppy is perhaps one of the most maddening episodes in the youngster's life for the trainer. Steady, insistent training coupled with kindness and encouragement put this part of his education across to him in the quickest, most satisfactory manner.

better to arrange for a professional trainer or school. If you plan to do it yourself, then be prepared to allot sufficient time.

The best type of training collar is a choke collar. This is a collar made of chain, with a ring where the lead is fastened. Slip the collar over the dog's head and attach the chain. A choke collar pulls tighter when you do, and loosens when you let up. It should be removed when not in use.

Use a sturdy collar so that it does not harm the dog. The lead can be of leather or chain. Be sure it is strong enough if you have an energetic puppy. When you attach the lead to the collar, have it pass over the dog's neck, not under it.

Suppose you collar your dog, attach the lead, and set out for a pleasant walk with him. The first thing he does is refuse to move. Or perhaps he moves too much, rushing off, and bounding in all

Serious obedience training should not be done before a dog is at least seven months old. A younger puppy's attention span is too short for him to derive any value from premature attempts at training, and can even hamper future training efforts.

The chain-choke collar is considered the most satisfactory collar for use in obedience training. It should not, however, be worn between training sessions and never on a working gun dog in the field. Some trainers prefer nylon chokes to chains.

directions until brought up by the lead. What now? Obviously, you and this whirling dervish cannot go parading down the street. In the first place, see that you are holding the lead and dog properly. The dog should be on your left side, the lead held in the right hand with your left hand available for extra strength and guidance. If your dog refuses to go with you on a leash, take him home. Let him get very hungry, then attach the leash and lead him to his food. If he associates good things with the collar and lead, he will be more cooperative the next time you plan an outing.

HEEL: What happens if he rushes off, pulling you along? We have seen any number of people being dragged along by their dogs, and this is surely a sign of poor training. If your puppy runs off, jerk the lead with the left hand and then stop, say **come,** and wait for his return. Praise him when he comes back. Sooner or later your dog will see that his wildness only results in stopping the walk altogether and general disapproval. Don't pull, incidentally, just jerk firmly but not unkindly. If you are full of admiration when he does come back, he will do it more willingly. Pretty soon, you can begin to use the word **heel** when he comes and walks at your side. If he stops, jerk him back firmly and say **heel.** If he bounds ahead, do the same thing and praise him when he comes back. Before you know it, he will be marching proudly by your side, the perfect gentleman. Of course, be prepared for little mishaps, such as the local cat, another dog, or an auto which may distract your dog before he has thoroughly mastered the commands to **come** and **heel.** Firmness and kindness should prevail, however.

Once you feel that he has thoroughly learned these lessons, try it off the lead. Hints to remember:

1. **Never work with your dog on any lesson until he has relieved himself.**
2. **Keep the lessons short. Fifteen minutes at a time is plenty.**
3. **Don't expect a dog to stay at "heel" for the whole walk; after all, he's a dog, isn't he, and a fellow needs a little time to play.**

ADVANCED TRAINING

SIT: Once your dog has learned the above, he is ready for the command to **sit.** You begin by adding the word **down** to his vocabulary. When he comes to you and jumps up, you say **down** and force

Teaching a dog to sit on command is accomplished by pulling up on the lead with the right hand and pushing down on the hindquarters with the left. The dog's name and the command "sit" should be given at the same time so the dog will associate the proper command with the appropriate action from him.

him down to the ground. Praise him when he obeys. Keep this up until he has learned not to jump up when you begin training.

The next step is **sit.** Stand the dog on your left side with the lead on, and tell him to **sit.** Follow words with action and push his hindquarters down. He may lie down all the way, and then you will just have to haul him up again and push down his hindquarters once more. Should he accidentally or actually begin to **sit,** praise him generously. You can appreciate what a hard lesson this is for him, for all he wants to do is jump up, lap your face and start playing.

To teach the dog to lie down at the command he must be in a sitting position and the handler must bear down on the lead while using the command "down."

Professional and amateur trainers always stress the importance of praise to the training program. A dog learns to associate praise with the performance of certain actions, and will always do them to please his handler. Praise is preferable to food reward as a dog might refuse to work without tidbits.

Repeat the lesson several times a day for short periods. Don't punish; just reward success or partial success with praise.

The command **lie down** can be taught in much the same way. Once the lesson is learned, try it without the lead.

STAY: Your dog now **comes, heels, sits down** and **lies down.** But the minute you leave, he does too! If you can teach him to **stay,** this will prove valuable. Suppose you want him to remain in the car while you shop, or with the baby carriage, or to stay quiet when a friend arrives. He must learn to stay in one place for a short period. Just as with the early lessons, use example and praise. As he learns, increase the scope of the command.

When you first command him to **stay,** sit him down, say **stay,** and then, holding the leash, walk around him or out towards the end of the lead. Of course, he will jump up and follow you. Don't yell at him; simply walk back and force him back into a sitting position, and then say **sit—stay.** You can also use a hand signal. Hold the palm of your hand in front of his nose when you say **sit— stay.** He will learn that as well as the word. After a while, he will get the idea and remain sitting while you walk around him.

When this lesson is learned, you can put the lead on the ground. Perhaps he is again nervous. Hold it with your foot. It won't be too long before you can leave him unattended and walk off. If he bolts after you, no praise, just repeat the whole lesson again. When you think he is sufficiently trained in the sit-stay position, then try distracting him by running off or bouncing a ball under his nose. Each time, if he gets up and starts off, begin again as before. Once the lesson is over and he has performed well, of course you can pat him and tell him how well he has done. Be careful not to pat him as soon as he has remained sitting for a moment, or he will think that the lesson's over.

The authors believe that if your dog is housebroken and can obey the commands to **come, heel, sit, lie down,** and **stay,** he will be completely manageable. You can then teach him tricks if you wish. If you so desire, teach your puppy to beg by propping him in the proper position and encouraging him to repeat this. Do not, however, allow him to use this cute trick to get food from you at the table. If you wish to reward him with a dog biscuit or candy at the time of the trick, fine, but if you feed him while you are eating because he begs so cutely, this cute trick will only become an chronic nuisance.

A phase of training not usually thought of as part of obedience, but very important nonetheless, is good traveling manners. Many dogs, particularly show animals and dogs that are regularly shot over, are trained to travel in crates. Such an arrangement is well-advised. The dogs are safer and more comfortable and the automobile is protected from dirt and mud of the field.

SPECIAL PROBLEMS

Some dogs, because of indifferent training or lack of training, develop problems which must be cured before they become acute and dangerous. The dog who jumps on people, barks all night, chases cars, and bites or steals food from the table must be retrained. **JUMPING ON PEOPLE:** There are several ways to combat this. If your dog will not obey your command to get down and not jump you can try the following: start by telling him **no** and putting him firmly on the floor. If he stays down, pat him. Some trainers advocate that when the dog jumps up you catch him with your knee so he falls back. This is unpleasant enough to stop him. Don't let him get the idea you are hurting him deliberately. As soon as he obeys, praise him.

CHASING CARS: There is no more dangerous and annoying habit for a dog than chasing cars. Dogs have been hit that way, and often in an effort to avoid the dog the driver endangers the lives of others. The best method is to start early and instill a proper fear of cars. Have another drive a car as you walk your dog along the road. When the car comes along, the driver is to give several loud blasts on the horn. At the same time you jerk your dog over to the side of the road. Repeat this several times, and the dog will instinctively move over to the side when he hears a car.

For the already delinquent dog, more severe methods must be used. The driver of the car can use a water pistol and squirt water at the dog as he jumps out at the car, or the driver can leap out of the car and yell loudly at the dog. Of course, you should be nearby in case the dog becomes frightened enough to attack the man. Once your dog shows that he has learned his lesson, he really deserves a medal! But a piece of dog candy will probably serve just as well.

BARKING: Many people purchase a dog for use as a watchdog. Persons on farms or valuable property, or those who are alone at night, may want a dog to warn them of approaching strangers. In these cases, the dog's bark is an asset. But the dog who barks all night, or barks at everyone regardless of who he is, or never stops barking at familiar people such as the paper boy, or garbage man, should be trained to be silent. Barking is a dog's way of talking and, of course, you don't want to completely muzzle him. But if you live in an apartment or populous neighborhood, a barking dog is very annoying and he often starts other dogs in the area baying. The resulting night-long chorus can cause troublesome relations with non-dog owners, and even some dog owners whose sleep is affected.

Prevention is the best cure, and you can start early after the basic lessons are completed. Begin by leaving your dog alone in his room. If he starts to bark, yell at him or knock loudly at the door. If he persists, go in and look your maddest. You can also be sly and pretend to go away. When he begins to howl, go through the routine again.

BITING: Dogs who bite are potentially dangerous. And dogs who continue to bite can be put away by order of a court if there have been complaints. First and foremost, do not encourage your young

Owning a dog that has had obedience training has many advantages. The most obvious is in having a well-mannered companion and a dog that engenders pride in his family and all who come in contact with him. An obedience trained dog can also be entered in AKC sponsored obedience trials to compete for prizes with other breeds.

puppy to bite people, even playfully (and that is what he is doing when he starts, *just playing*). If he must chew on something, get him some inanimate object such as a toy or a rawhide bone. If he continues to bite, express your disapproval. He may need more severe punishment. Hold his jaw shut until he stops or slap him gently on the muzzle. Be sure to fondle him afterwards if he obeys. If you do not tease your dog, he will be less inclined to bite. A dog doesn't like to be poked or interrupted when he is eating. His instincts may cause him to growl and defend himself. But a dog should not growl at his master; firm treatment will tell him so.

FURNITURE SITTING: Do you come home and find your dog in your favorite chair? Next thing you know, he will have your slippers and your paper too. This is a habit which should be broken, unless you don't mind cleaning bills. Remove the dog firmly. Perhaps you can provide a comfortable spot in the living room for him so he can be with you. If it continues, some trainers advocate setting a little mousetrap under some paper on the chair. The noise will frighten him off. This can be used, but if you are inclined to worry over noses and toes, try a child's squeaky toy or crackly paper.

FOOD STEALING: Dogs who steal food are both impolite and dangerous to themselves. If your dog does take food he may be eating the wrong foods and ruining that careful diet you prepared, or perhaps he may eat a poisonous substance. Train him to take food only from his dinner plate, at his dinner hour, or on special occasions when you offer a treat. A loud **no** when your dog reaches for forbidden food and general disapproval may work, but you can also try pepper on the enticing tidbit.

Dogs sometimes have other annoying habits which can be cured using much the same methods described above. Kindness and consistency are important and reward for good behavior will reinforce your dog's good habits and discourage bad ones.

SPECIAL TRAINING FOR SHOWING

There are many excellent books on the market describing the type of training you need for Bench Shows and Obedience Trials. One highly recommended publication is **How to Housebreak and Train Your Dog** by Arthur Leibers. This booklet, in addition to describing basic training, also offers a section of the special training needed to qualify for the Obedience Trials sponsored by the AKC and affiliated clubs.

The title of Companion Dog (C.D.) in the novice class is awarded if your dog can earn at least 50% of the points for each test and a total of 170 for the trial in three different shows.

Maximum
Score

35	1. Heel on leash
30	2. Stand for examination by the judge
45	3. Heel free—off leash
30	4. Recall (come on command)
30	5. Sit for one minute (handler in ring)
30	6. Sit for three minutes (handler in ring)

200

When this hurdle is passed, your dog is ready to earn his C.D.X. (X for Excellent). This requires that he must qualify in three shows.

Maximum
Score

40	1. Heel free
30	2. Drop on recall
25	3. Retrieve on flat (ground)
35	4. Retrieve over an obstacle
20	5. Broad jump
25	6. Sit for three minutes (handler out of ring)
25	7. Sit for five minutes (handler out of ring)

200

He can then enter the Utility Class and compete in tests including scent discrimination, signal exercises, directed jumping and group exams. The final test is a tracking exercise, and with that he earns his U.D.T. (T for Tracking), the Ph.D. of the Obedience Class.

The special training needed for Obedience competition which is described in Mr. Liebers' book can be taught by a professional trainer or in a class.

German Pointers have little trouble in learning to perform the jumping exercises that are a part of AKC competition. The dog should be taught to "sit-stay" at heel before being given the command to jump.

PROFESSIONAL TRAINERS

Many dogs are sent by their owners to professional trainers. This is essential when there is no one at home to supervise a dog and teach him his *p's* and *q's*. Or perhaps the dog is quite large and active and a trainer is necessary. Another reason might be that you plan to show the dog or place him in Obedience Trials, and want professional help. If your dog has been badly trained or frightened,

Many times the handler will have to accompany his dog over a low jump in the beginning stages of training. This situation does not last long though and before long the dog will take a jump by himself with ease.

Most obedience exercises finish with the dog sitting squarely in front of the handler. When the dog is sitting properly the handler will command "heel," and the dog will turn and sit at the handler's left side.

you may want such a person to straighten him out. Be prepared for fees which may be high. Your veterinarian or breeder can probably recommend a trainer, or you can look through the many dog publications. Be sure when you take the dog home that you receive full instructions on how to handle him and the proper words to use.

TRAINING CLASSES

Many communities sponsor classes for dogs. The local A.S.P.C.A. or humane society may hold inexpensive classes, or the local dog club may sponsor one. The cost of the classes is generally modest— about $10.00. You will long remember attending the first class of the year in your home town. What bedlam, what a commotion! People and dogs will be pulled all over the place. But by the time the class is under way and in the following weeks, calm, more or less, will reign. You can check with friends or with your veterinarian to see if the classes are effective and the teacher qualified. But don't think that all you will have to do is to attend classes and your

An obedience dog should be taught jumping starting with low hurdles, and gradually brought up to jumping over higher obstacles. The AKC determines the height of the jump based on the shoulder height of each competitor.

The ability to retrieve is instinctive with sporting breeds. It is only necessary for the trainer to set the pattern for the form and style of retrieving used in regular obedience competition.

dog will be the perfect lady or gentleman. You must be prepared to practice what you *both* have learned when you go home. The advantages of a training class for dogs are that you do obtain the services of a professional who can teach you how to do it, and that the dog becomes accustomed to other dogs and strangers.

Most dogs prefer people to other dogs; they are truly man's companion. But they must learn to respect other dogs and not fight with them. Fights are dangerous both to dogs and the bystanders. If your dog does get into a dog fight, don't step in unless you are prepared to get bitten or scratched. He may be so excited that your dog may not even know you. Cold water from a hose is often effective. If you have guts, you can wade in and grab the most aggressive dog. Hold him tightly by the collar or the throat until he is half choked. He will generally let go. Neighbors who cooperate and keep their dogs in, or penned in runs, rarely have these problems.

A gun dog that does not retrieve the game the hunter has shot is of little value in the field. Marking ability, courage, and ability to handle shot game well are all indicators of a dog's positive retrieving style.

SPECIAL TRAINING FOR THE GERMAN POINTER

German Shorthaired and Wirehaired Pointers are hunting dogs. Although many people own Pointers that are strictly housepets and companions, their usefulness in the field has made them attractive to hunters and favorites in field trials. This book cannot give you the fine points of training for the hunting dog, but as mentioned before, there are many books and magazines which have detailed information, and we recommend that you consult these sources for help. There are also many trainers who specialize in this area, as well as gun clubs where you can obtain help and information from hunting enthusiasts.

Those who hunt in areas of rough country or unusually heavy cover might choose to hunt over a German Wirehaired Pointer. The breed's soft, thick undercoat keeps the dog warm even in foulest weather. His water-resistant, harsh outercoat retards dampness and the effects of hunting in heavy brambles or thorns.

The German Shorthaired Pointer makes a good hunting companion for the sportsman who wants the field ability of the English Pointer, but in an animal that is more of a personal shooting dog. Continental Pointers have always been taught to work close to the gun and do better as part of a family than as inmates of a large kennel.

However, there are several things you can do to prepare your dog for such specialized training. For this early training, you will need a choke collar, a 25-foot lead of rope and a whistle.

"COME", "GO", "WHOA"

These three words are the most important in your dog's hunting vocabulary. They are taught in conjunction with both hand signals and whistle blasts.

Come: The first training you give your dog is **come**. This is essential for hunting dogs, which must be taught to obey you scrupulously. Accompany this instruction with a long blast on the whistle and a wave of the hand signaling him to come in.

Go: The second word is **go** which sends your dog off into the field or further on when he has stopped. Two short blasts are the signal for this command.

Whoa: This word is the typical hunter's word to bring the dog to a halt. This can be taught with the long rope. Collar and leash the dog and then let him out to run. Then call **whoa.** If he doesn't stop (just out of curiosity perhaps) he will soon be brought up short by the rope. A couple of experiences in which he lands head over heels and he will know the meaning of the word.

With all these words, lavish praise is in order when your dog obeys you. Most dogs relish this form of reward far more than other more concrete presents, but a dog candy or bit of liver helps too.

The first step in forming a finished gundog is to steady him when birds are flushed. This is done with the use of the check cord as shown below.

Water retrieves are usual for any German Pointer. While not a specialist at this work, he gives a good account of himself when a bird has been shot over any body of water.

RETRIEVING

One of the attractions that the German Shorthaired Pointer has for hunters is his versatility. He not only points but also retrieves in all manner of land cover, as well as in water.

Retrieving is natural with many dogs. Toss a ball and they will bound off and bring it back. This is annoying to small fry playing baseball, but is an asset in a hunting dog. If you wish the training to be more formal, you can use a dummy (called a buck) such as a thick dowel or rolled up magazine. Show it to the dog and tease him a bit until he grabs it. Then ask him to **give** it to you. He may object, but if you blow into his nostrils he will relinquish it to you. Soon you can toss it a short distance away and order him to **fetch.** When he returns to you, tell him to **give.** Some trainers suggest that you pinch his ear if your dog is reluctant to give up his prize.

For serious hunters, retrieving is essential. Some dogs must be taught to retrieve if their natural instincts are not strong in this area. Force retrieving is best taught by a professional handler.

After a hunting dog is proficient with retrieving the dummy, he graduates to dead birds. He should be trained to come back in and sit in front of you with the bird in his mouth, until the command to **give.**

POINTING

Pointing is another natural instinct in hunting dogs. They are bred for this, but like other instincts it must be nurtured and encouraged

Many trainers like to start a young dog's bird work either with live or dead pigeons. Introduction to birds is a very critical phase of a field dog's education. Too-early exposure and possible encounters with strong cripples may ruin an otherwise fine animal for life.

Before introducing a dog to birds he should be trained to retrieve the dummy. This is usually a canvas boat bumper or article of similar shape and size. Sometimes it is treated with bird scent so as to make the changeover from dummy to game smoother.

The end result of training, a capable, finished shooting companion, is well worth the painstaking efforts at training. There are few things that are as satisfying as shaping a young animal into a priceless hunting companion and sporting friend.

and properly instilled. Some trainers advocate that for some time young puppies should be allowed freedom in the fields, where they can run about, sniffing and even rousing up a few scared butterflies and robins. Others advocate "yard" training at an early age. Without time to play, some of your dog's zest for hunting may be lost.

At some time during this play, you will see your dog stiffen when he scents a bird. This may last only a second or so. You can now begin more formal training. The goal is a steady point (called staunchness) which is not broken until the dog is ordered to go on. Some dogs will break at the sound of the gun, but others won't. Pointing can be encouraged with rope training or out in the field with other experienced dogs.

Using a rope, let your dog see or scent a small freshly killed bird. He will probably attempt to point, but when he breaks the point to go after the bird, pull on the rope and hold him back. When he gets out into the field, you cannot expect that he will point his first (or even second, third, or fourth) covey without flushing the birds. After a while, however, he should learn to stand staunchly. Experience will teach this. Some dogs have been known to remain staunch for as long as an hour. Lots of encouragement and praise will reward your dog for all his efforts.

GUN SHOTS

Some dogs are "born" gun-shy, and retraining takes much time and effort. If you intend to hunt with your dogs, however, they must be trained to stand at gunshots. Most trainers advocate that this training begin early and that it be associated with pleasant things like eating. When your dog is still very young, you can begin by shooting

A gun dog that is steady to shot and wing is of far greater value than an unsteady animal. Steady to shot and wing means that the dog will not break when birds are flushed or when a shot is fired. He will wait for a command from the hunter before going in and making a retrieve.

Beauty, brains, and useful versatility have always been the hallmarks of both German Pointers. This exquisite Shorthair bitch exemplifies the classic flow and grace that spell sporting beauty without a peer wherever men and dogs join in the hunt.

A soft mouth is essential to any dog that handles game. The dog must not chew or otherwise mutilate the bird that has been shot.

No sporting dog should be apprehensive of the sight or sound of guns. Occasionally gunshyness is a hereditary factor, but in most cases it results from poor training and poor management.

Good friends, good dogs and a full game bag at the end of the day are keys to hunting's greatest pleasures. German Pointers, of both coats contribute substantially to the American gunner and his active sporting scene.

off a cap pistol at a distance when he approaches his dinner plate. Of course, he will look up, but if you continue to act unconcerned, he will get down to business. Gradually, you can come nearer at each feeding time until you are able to fire the gun off practically under his nose. When you do get out into the fields, you can use a blank cartridge pistol and fire over his head while he is pointing, but do not attempt this until he had made several successful points and is accustomed to all the activity and excitement in the field.

Good hunting dogs should be taught to remain steady until ordered to "fetch". This is called "steady to shot and wing" and is one of the nicer finishing touches in a fine hunting dog. This can be taught with use of the long check rope.

There are many other fine points which professional handlers and trainers can teach your dog. A well-trained hunting dog is a joy to own and can afford you many hours of pleasure. But even non-hunting dogs should be well trained—happy and obedient, not cowed or vicious. This can best be accomplished by training them with kindness, firmness, consistency and the proper rewards for good behavior.

Chapter X

Kennels, Runs and Bedding

A man's home is his castle and a dog's home is his kennel. But your dog depends on *you* to provide him with clean, comfortable quarters.

The first thing you should do when your dog arrives is show him where he lives. This may be a spot in the house or a kennel outside. When your dog comes into your home, remember that he is in a strange place, far from his family. Show him his new home, but don't just leave him there and depart, turning off the light or closing the door. He's young, probably frightened and very lonely. A little love and affection and time for him to get acquainted and sniff about his bed or kennel and he'll settle in fast enough.

If you live in an apartment, he will live indoors. If possible, choose a spot which is convenient for the whole family, where the dog can have some privacy. If you live in a house you have the option of having an indoor or outdoor pet. Most small dogs are more comfortable indoors, where they are less affected by the weather. A large active dog like the Shorthair or Wirehair Pointer is better off outdoors in a comfortable house with a large run. But whatever type of housing you provide for your pet, it must be clean, airy, warm in winter, ventilated in summer and large enough to accommodate your dog. The most important rule is that kennels and bedding must be kept clean and dry. Dirty living quarters can harbor many germs, especially worm eggs, which are passed on to the dog.

When should a dog be outside? Small puppies, warmed by their mothers, can huddle outside a kennel in quite cold weather, but if it is very cold, they should be inside. Older dogs with thick coats and hardy dispositions can stay outdoors. Indeed, it is dangerous to keep an outdoor dog inside for too long, for he then becomes more susceptible to cold.

Well-constructed kennel runs should be large enough for their occupants to exercise in freely, strong enough to withstand wear from natural elements and continual use, and high enough to preclude escape in the event that a given dog is so inclined.

PROFESSIONAL KENNELS

When you consider a kennel for boarding or hospitalization there are certain factors in kennel construction you should note, to see if the kennel is satisfactory.

A good kennel is large and airy. The ceiling is high, with good ventilation. The kennel contains pens and sleeping areas which take into consideration the size of the dogs they accommodate, as well as separate quarters for sick dogs and whelping. Each dog should have his own sleep space, but outdoor pens can be shared for exercise. The kennel should be clean. Today some kennels use wirebottomed pens, especially for smaller dogs. These have the advantage of being easier to keep clean and less likely to harbor germs. A wirebottomed pen is made up of two parts: a box for sleeping and an outdoor area for play and exercise. A hinged door provides room to clean and show the dogs. Contrary to what many people think, the wire bottom does not injure the dog's feet.

OUTDOOR KENNELS

Most people are concerned with housing a single dog, or two at the most. Outdoor housing can be purchased. If you do buy a doghouse, be sure it is solidly contructed, easy to clean and adquately ventilated. It must be large enough! A small puppy can grow into a large dog. Veterinarians recommend that the sleeping area, your dog's bed-

Kennel dogs can be watered easily by supplying this from a hose in bucket receptacles in each run. This is not always practical in areas with severe winters as water in a bucket will freeze solid in very cold weather.

room, be at least 2 times the width of the grown dog and $1\frac{1}{2}$ times his height.

Place the kennel in a spot that has some shade as well as sun. If possible, set it several inches off the ground so that moisture and rodents do not affect your dog.

A homemade kennel can be constructed, using old lumber and material from your workshop. But whether you purchase of build your kennel, the following plan is recommended.

Your doghouse should, for the most dog-comfort, follow the two-room plan—one room for sleeping and an entry way. A porch is nice also, so your dog can watch the world go by without having to lie on damp ground. If you live in a cold climate the kennel should be insulated. A hinged roof provides better ventilation, and greater ease of cleaning. You can also provide a slightly raised curbing at the entry of the bedroom, to hold the bedding in place.

To keep the kennel clean, scrub it with water and a mild disinfectant. Your dog is proud of his home and not likely to mess it up, but

Stools in a kennel should be picked up and removed every day. This is for the general cleanliness, well being of the dogs and for the appearance of the area when visitors come to call.

Scrupulous hygiene is very important in keeping a kennel of dogs or only one dog. The kennel owner should make sure that all runs and boxes are always kept clean and that periodic disinfecting should be done for the entire place.

if he has been sick or just wormed, be sure that the kennel is thoroughly scrubbed and disinfected, and the bedding burned.

The best type of bedding for an outdoor kennel is cedar shavings. They are easily purchased in any pet store, and they smell sweet and clean. Be sure to change the bedding occasionally.

INDOOR SLEEPING QUARTERS

A dog raised indoors should also have a private place. Sometimes, this is in the cellar, if it is warm and dry. Many people use the family room, which has less valuable furniture and rugs than other rooms in the home.

Most people who provide for their dogs indoors purchase a bed. A trip to the neighborhood pet stores will show the number of commercially available sizes and styles. The two major types are wicker and metal, and the type you choose may depend on where you plan to put the bed. Wicker is more attractive and will provide a neat, handsome addition to your kitchen, family room or bedroom. The metal bed, while not as attractive, is sturdier. Be sure that the metal is painted with non-lead-based paint. If you are worried about your puppy chewing up the wicker and getting splinters, there is a bitter but harmless preparation on the market which can be rubbed on the wicker to discourage chewing.

Two types of filling are commonly used for mattresses: cedar shavings and cotton. The mattresses with cedar shavings can be changed, which may be necessary if you have a small puppy. It may be better, while the dog is young, to provide him with an old blanket which he can chew to rags. But beware: many dogs become attached to their blanket and won't give it up.

RUNS FOR POINTERS

If you live in the city, you will naturally take your dog for walks on a leash. Both master (or mistress) and dog can get their daily constitutional this way. In the suburbs or country, however, the best way to exercise your dog is to provide an outdoor exercise area such as a run, or tie-out stakes. One of the problems of the country dog is road safety. Since it is possible to run free—either singly or with groups of other dogs—speeding motorists, wild animals and other sources of danger can jeopardize his life. The considerate dog owner will provide a place for his dog to exercise when he can't take him out on a leash. The run should be as large as possible, up to 20 x 40 feet. A rectangular shape is most convenient. It should have a strong wire fence at least four feet high, with a gate fastened with a spring hook. If there is no wooden or iron top rail, the dog will be less likely to try jumping over. Dogs usually aim at something when they jump, and if there is only a thin strand of wire at the top he will have no target.

There are many opinions as to the best flooring for runs and kennels. The one basic principle on which all agree is that the material should be easy to keep clean. Some experts recommend concrete, smoothly troweled and finished. Others contend that this harbors worm eggs and is very hard to keep clean. Sand is often recommended, but the same argument is used against sand. If your run is not permanent, grass is satisfactory, but you must expect that it will be considerably trampled.

Some dog owners have the kennel and run together. Others put their dogs into the run only for exercise. Protect your dog from the hot sun by providing some shade if there is no doghouse. You can place the run near or under some trees, or construct a platform for protection.

Be sure you provide water also. There is nothing like a fresh drink of water to cool a fellow off after a hot run around the exercise area. If you do have a run, no matter how large it is, don't leave your pet in for very long stretches. Dogs, like people, get bored, and your dog likes a change of scenery, even if he only goes into the house or his kennel.

Good kennel management manifests itself in the look of sleek, well-tended animals. These two puppies are obvious examples of knowledge-able husbandry.

Proper management has many dividends for the conscientious kennel operator. Show animals are too valuable to be maintained on a "second-class" regime. They will reflect their good care in themselves, the young they produce and the wins they bring home.

The above points also apply to tie-out stakes, which should have water and protection from the sun, as well as adequate room to exercise.

The major points to remember about housing and runs is that they must be clean and comfortable. This will keep your dog healthier and happier also.

Chapter XI

Grooming and Exercising

There is nothing more attractive than an alert, healthy and well-groomed Shorthair or Wirehair—with his well-groomed coat and athletic stance. In other chapters we have emphasized the importance of proper diet and medical care. This chapter will show you how to make your dog's appearance reflect the care you have given him.

Grooming cannot start too early in a dog's life. The puppy can be started with a soft brush and worked up to the grooming implements normally used on grown dogs. In this way he is not likely to resent standard grooming procedures when he is big enough to give an operator a difficult time of it.

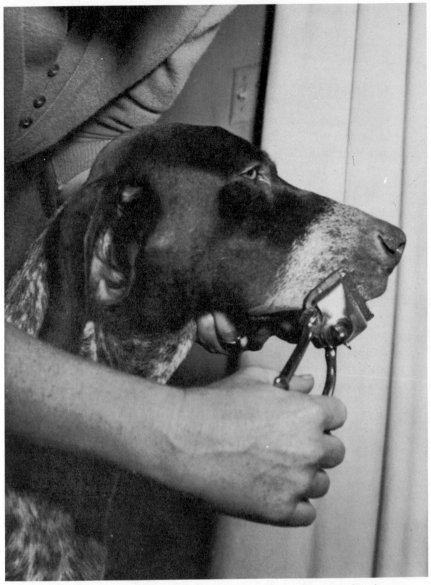

For the show ring grooming procedures go a bit farther than for the pet or field dog. A scissor, electric clipper, or, as shown, a hand clipper is used to trim off facial whiskers and other hairs that take away from the desired sleek outline of the German Shorthair.

As dog owners we know that both we and our dogs delight in compliments. By regular grooming and careful provision for exercise, we can doubly reward our pet with well-earned praise and a happy, healthy life.

GROOMING

Grooming is a matter of habit for both dog and master. Regular grooming should be pleasure for both; and it will be, if your pet is accustomed to his weekly combing and brushing. Start grooming early, be kind but firm, and you will find that he welcomes his grooming sessions.

TRAINING FOR PLEASURABLE GROOMING

The first thing to teach your dog is *patience* during grooming. Don't allow him to "act up" at this time—after all, who's the boss? He must learn to stand quietly while being combed, brushed, trimmed or clipped. If you begin when your puppy is quite small, he will soon learn to enjoy grooming. Some breeders start to brush the pups while they are still in the nest and have little difficulty when the puppies grow up.

The easiest place to groom a dog is on a table or bench, and you

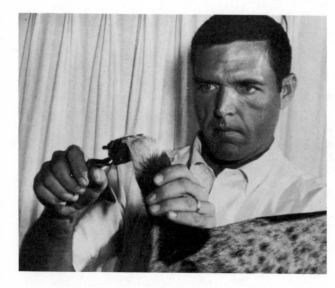

Part of show grooming is in removing any stray hairs that may otherwise mar the smooth, continuous line from neck to stern.

190

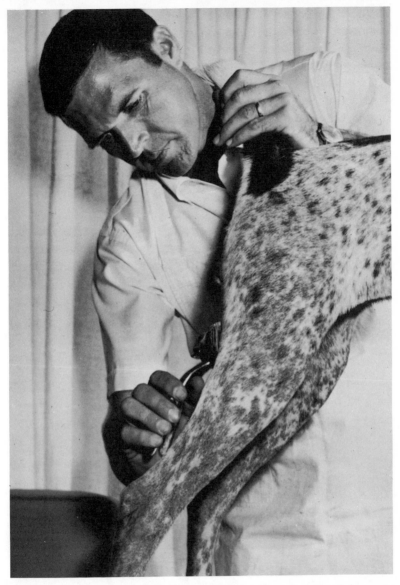

The hair on the back of the stifle grows longer than the rest of the coat. This hair should be cleaned so that a smooth appearance will catch the judge's eye.

should train your Pointer to jump onto a bench, preferably on command. **Table** is the command used by most breeders; if your dog enjoys his beauty session, he will respond eagerly. For greater ease groom your Pointer on a bench.

At the start, if you or your pet are nervous, attach the leash to a hook above the table or bench, which will hold him in place. If your dog is very young or still unsure, start your grooming activities (brushing, combing, etc.) from the rear, so that he becomes accustomed to the sensations gradually.

YOUR POINTER'S COAT

A dog is the direct reflection of his heredity, diet and general health, shown to his best by grooming. Proper care of the coat will insure that it is shiny and free from parasites, coat or skin ailments.

The skin and coat of all dogs have certain general characteristics in common, regardless of the breed. The skin contains oil glands

Judicious trimming and grooming is the key to making a Shorthair ring-ready. It is only for the operator to refine the gifts nature has given to the individual animal to make a show dog.

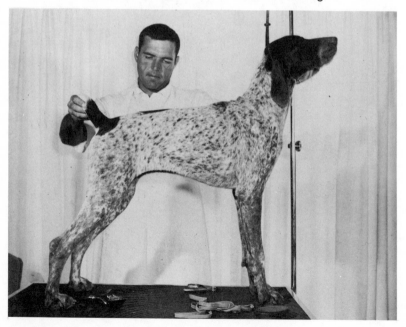

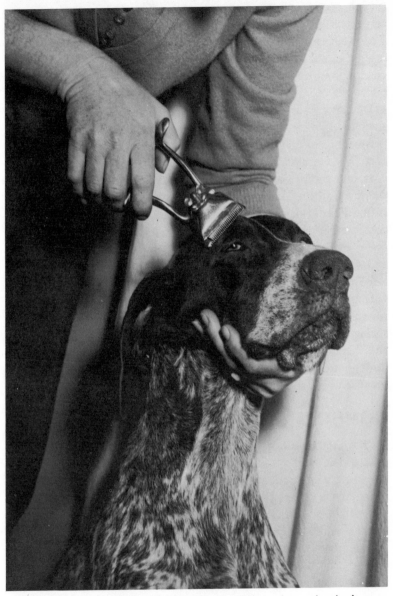

The operator must not forget to trim the feelers above the dog's eyes.
A foreign picture is created if the muzzle is well barbered but whiskers
are still seen at the dog's brow.

(which secrete oil to keep the coat shiny and waterproof), the sebaceous glands (related to hair growth) and some sweat glands. The sebaceous glands secrete a waxy substance called sebum, which coats the hair as it grows. It is this substance which you often find coating your dog's collar, and sometimes accounts for that "doggy" odor.

Do not be surprised if your dog occasionally develops dandruff, since the *skin* continually sheds and renews itself.

Most breeds of dogs have two coats—a soft undercoat and an outercoat. The German Shorthaired Pointer has a hard, shiny, shorthaired coat, and a very short, dense undercoat. This is especially useful in the field, where longer coats attract burrs and tangles. The Wirehaired Pointer has both an undercoat and an outercoat. The undercoat is either dense or thin, depending on the season. Some Wirehairs, however, have little or no undercoat. The outercoat is straight, harsh and wiry, although some dogs have relatively smooth coats resembling the Shorthair's.

Dogs usually shed once a year, but some seem to shed all year round. We know that the increasing length of daylight hours in spring is one factor causing shedding. Dogs living primarily indoors and therefore exposed to artificial light may shed more often or even throughout the year. Fortunately, the Shorthair sheds very little because of his short coat.

COMBING AND BRUSHING

Your dog should be groomed at least once a week, or preferably once a day, and you will find that he gets much pleasure from the grooming which will give your dog his shining look. The Shorthair is one of the easiest dogs to keep neat and well-groomed, since he is naturally so. Most Shorthairs need not be combed before they are brushed, unless they are very dirty. A suitable sturdy comb, one which will not break or bend, can be obtained in any pet store. When combing shorthaired dogs, be careful not to scrape the skin. Mats can can be teased apart; the use of a little oil will simplify this task. If you cut the mats out, you leave a bald spot which is unsightly. Burrs should also be removed without the use of scissors.

After any necessary combing, brush your Shorthair carefully. A natural bristle brush is ideal. Brush in the direction of the coat until it is smooth and shining. A hound glove may then be used to give an extra gleam for special occasions. These brushes can be obtained in the pet shop. Both comb and brush should be cleaned after each use and then stored in the open to air.

Because of his coat, the Wirehaired Pointer often picks up burrs and mats while in the field. These should be gently teased out. Comb and brush his coat as described above.

NAIL CLIPPING

Long nails can force a dog's toes outward and permanently affect his stance if this occurs during puppyhood. If you enjoy an occasional romp with your pet, you will also find it safer for both you and your clothing to keep his nails clipped. As a part of your dog's regular checkup the veterinarian can clip his nails. Ask him to show how to do this chore for future reference. If you purchase a good pair of scissors, you can do it yourself. The part you must trim is the hook, the section of the nail which curves downward. Be careful not to cut

Proper care of the nails is essential to the well-being of all dogs, but for a show animal the nails must be short and the foot must present a tight, well-knuckled appearance.

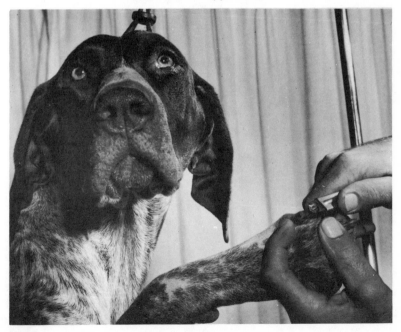

into the vein as it bleeds profusely. In small pups or light-haired dogs, the line where the vein begins is easy to spot. In dark-colored nails this is more difficult to see, but shining a flashlight under the nail will help you find the vein.

Are you nervous about clipping? Then file the nails. A good wooden file can do an excellent job of shortening nails, or you can use the file to finish off the job of clipping. When you first begin to file, you will have to bear down quite hard to break the hard, polished surface of the nail. Draw the file in one direction, from the top of the nail downward, in a round stroke to the end of the nail.

If you do accidentally cut into the dog's vein, it's not fatal—bandage the foot until bleeding has stopped, and apply a styptic pencil. The bandage will keep the blood from spattering around.

Most people find that their dogs need nail trimming about once in two months. If your dog walks mostly on concrete sidewalks, his nails will wear down naturally and he may never need nail clipping.

All long hair should be cleaned from the underside and special attention should be given to the longer hair that grows at the tuck-up.

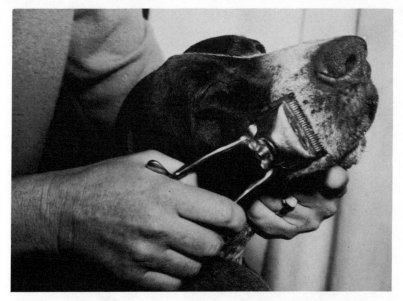

While the hand clipper is commonly used for trimming the Shorthair, the Wirehair should be trimmed with finger and thumb or a stripping comb. The skull and ears should be cleaned and brows should be left over the eyes. The feet should carry no excess hair and rest of the dog is tidied of long hair that takes away from the outline.

CLIPPING

The Shorthair does not need clipping but occasionally (especially if you show him) he does need a bit of scissoring around the legs, just enough to trim off the straggly hairs and make the coat neater. Hairs around the muzzle and ears can also be trimmed off with a scissors for a "sharper" look.

TEETH

A little care goes a long way. Tartar is your dog's worst tooth problem. Dog biscuits, and bones made from nylon or hide are good toothbrushes, although the authors do not recommend meat bones, which may splinter. If heavy tartar does form, it can best be removed by a veterinarian.

Sometimes, puppy teeth do not fall out on schedule, and they must be pulled to make room for the second teeth. Your veterinarian can check this for you when your puppy is examined.

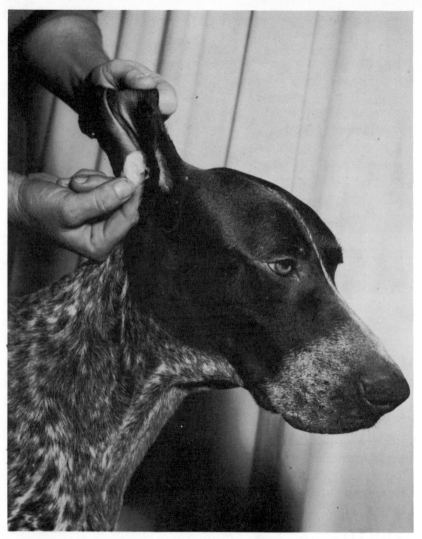

Regular care of the ears is another grooming essential. It is somewhat easier to keep after a Shorthair's ears, but with regular care ears are not a problem with either coat type.

If your dog has "bad breath", check the condition of his mouth and also his diet. There is even a breath deodorizer available at your pet shop to make your dog more "sociable".

EARS

Veterinarians advise that you leave a dog's ears alone. More damage is done by probing than disease. If your dog's ears appear dirty or full of wax, you can clean them out gently with a cotton-tipped swab dipped in warm water. But do not thrust the swab into the ear canal. Some dogs have hair growing in the ear canal. This is usually quite easy to remove. Use your fingers or a forceps to pull it gently out. Do not use force.

At some time, you may see your dog scratching his ears along the ground or shaking his head violently. He may have some irritation, such as a canker, in his ear. Check with your veterinarian. You can relieve the condition by filling the ear with mineral oil. To do this, put the dog on a table or bench, hold the ear flap so that you can see the ear canal, and pour the oil into the ear until it is filled. Then massage the base of the ear, wiping up the oil that escapes. This

The dog that is hunted should have his pads examined after each expedition. Seeds, burrs and other natural material found there should be promptly removed for the dog's comfort and safety. Left intact they can create a nasty and painful infection later on.

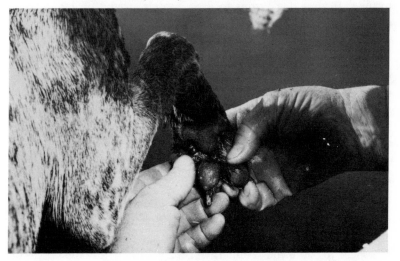

treatment will dissolve wax and help clean the ear out. For more serious ear problems, your veterinarian should be consulted.

EYES

The eyes rarely need grooming care. If they exude a little matter, wipe them out with a piece of moist cotton. If you use your Pointer for hunting, check his eyes after each trip. Hunting dogs often pick up weed seeds or bits of dirt. Wash the eyes with a boric acid solution.

FEET

Hunting dogs sometimes pick up thorns or tiny stones in their foot pads, and these can be quite painful. Check your dog's feet after field trips and remove thorns, stones, etc. A dab of antiseptic is added protection when you remove thorns.

ANAL GLANDS

The anal glands are two glands situated on either side of the anus. They appear to serve the same purpose as those of a skunk, and they also leave an unpleasant odor. If a dog is extremely frightened or the loser in a fight, he may release the contents of the glands. However, if the glands are not naturally discharged, they may become enlarged and infected. To prevent infection they must be emptied from time to time. If your dog begins to drag himself around on his tail and there is a swollen appearance around the anus, check the glands. If you can feel two hard lumps, it's time for action.

Before you empty the glands, stand the dog in a tub or arm yourself with a big wad of tissues or cotton, as the liquid you will extract is quite smelly. Try not to get any on your hands. With one hand hold the tail up. With the other, using the thumb and middle finger, gently squeeze each lump up and outward. If this does not empty them, consult your veterinarian. He may have to perform the task.

BATHS

To bathe or not to bathe, that is the question! The best rule of thumb is to bathe your dog only when he cannot be cleaned by any other means. If you comb and brush your dog regularly, you will find little need to bathe your Pointer. Of course, he may love dust baths or

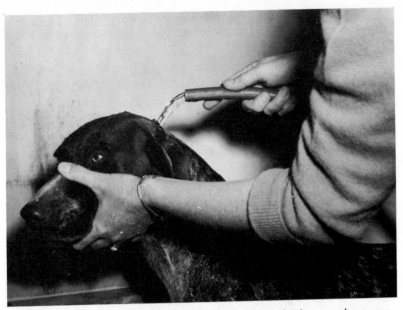

A dog should not be bathed too often, but proper bath procedures are handy to know. In the upper photo the operator is hosing the animal down to get off surface dirt and oil. Below the operator is applying a shampoo made specifically for use on dogs. Human hair products should be avoided as they are usually too harsh.

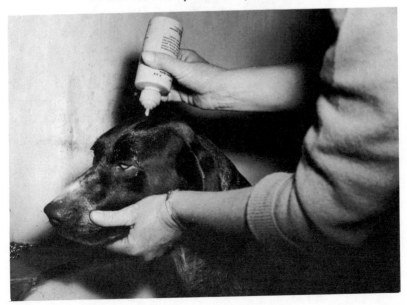

the feel of paint or tar, and then you will have to resort to a bath. Baths should be held to a minimum, because too-frequent bathing dries out the oil glands, and the skin and coat become very dry.

Puppies often need more baths than fully grown (and trained) dogs. No matter how young your puppy is, he won't be harmed by a tub bath. However, we recommend that you plug his ears with cotton and put a drop or two of mineral oil in his eyes. This is all the protection your dog needs, if you use the techniques described below.

Soaps: There are many soap preparations on the market for your pet's bath. One of the best is a 50% solution of coconut oil which you further dilute with water before use. You can also use almost any detergent found in the pet stores. The best shampoo is "pet quality" as "human quality" is too harsh to use on dogs.

Sometimes a bath after a hunting trip is a good idea, especially if the dog has been involved in a number of water retrieves.

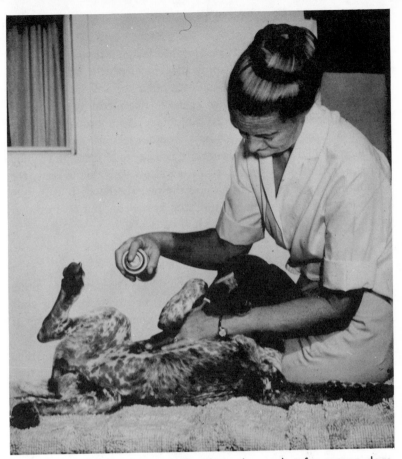

Many dry bath products are offered on the market for use on dogs. They are a handy aid for cleaning dogs between baths, and many even contain vermicidal ingredients to retard parasites.

Other types of soap are called *dry-bath* soaps; these do not need water. They are either powder-based and contain flea killing insecticides, or aerosol spray soaps. The powder types are rubbed in and then brushed out. The sprays are sprayed over the dog and then rubbed in and toweled out. Most of the dry baths are excellent, but more expensive than regular soaps. Still another new type of shampoo has been developed, a tearless shampoo which eliminates eye problems.

Experimentation with the different varieties and brands of commercially available dog soaps will enable you to find exactly the right kind for your dog.

Technique: Most dogs are best washed in a tub. If your dog won't get into a tub of water, use a spray attachment which you can attach to the faucet. Pour a line of soap down the middle of the dog's back and lather it in. Work it in so that the dog's coat is completely covered with soap. Rinse and resoap. Then rinse thoroughly so that no trace of soap remains. If you wish, you can then use a dip to bring out the color highlights. Now your dog is ready to be dried and a good rub is in order. A soft towel is fine, and now your dog is ready for anything—a show, or a trip around the neighborhood. If it is very warm outside, let the dog finish drying in the sun, but be sure that he is *completely* dry before letting him outdoors.

PARASITES

Lice and fleas are discussed in Chapter XII, Diseases, but routine control of these annoying pests can be part of grooming. Bathe your pet with any of the preparations for flea control on the market if you suspect that he has fleas. And be sure to give the kennel and bedding a good bath also. Many professional kennel owners deflea their dogs' quarters regularly. If you keep both dog and bed free from these pests, there is less chance of severe infestations.

DOGGY ODOR

As your dog grows older, he will smell "doggier". An occasional bath, plus a dusting of antiseptic powder for parasites will help. Check his anal glands and teeth and see that the diet is proper and there will be less odor.

Your dog's collar can also be a source of odor. When you wash your pet, remove the collar and give it a bath too. Scrape off the accumulated dirt and wax and clean with alcohol. Then air it out and oil it well before putting it back on the dog.

SKUNKS

If your dog tangles with a skunk, the skunk will probably be the winner. Unfortunately, both you and the dog are the losers. Don't take off in the other direction when he comes home after any such encounter. Wash him thoroughly and put him near the radiator or out in the sun. The odor will disappear in time. Some people advocate washing the animal in tomato juice, but we have not tried this technique as yet.

PAINT

The best chemical with which to remove paint is kerosene. Rub off the paint as soon as possible with a cloth dipped in kerosene and then wash it off well. Kerosene may burn an animal's skin, so apply it with care.

Try to keep your dog from chewing on the paint which is on his fur, as it may contain poisonous substances.

TAR

If the city has been tarring your road, you can be sure that your dog will have investigated. If he comes home with tar on his feet or

A dog, in the normal course of events, can get into many things that create a cleaning job for the owner. The best way to handle this matter is to have a reliable dog that has been trained to avoid "unsanitary pitfalls" as much as possible.

coat, use the same method as noted above (paint). It may take several treatments. Fortunately, the Shorthair's short, hard coat minimizes paint and tar problems.

EXERCISE

Exercise is "doing what comes naturally" for most Pointers. If left completely free, your dog could probably be found running over the fields and woods, happily pointing any birds which come into his path. But civilization—our crowded urban areas—and the special requirements of breeding and control impose restrictions on your dog's exercise area.

The Pointer in the city should be exercised regularly by walking, which he will greatly enjoy. Most cities and town require that dogs be on a leash when out in the street, but this should not prevent your dog from getting full benefit from his walk. He can then get the rest of his exercise in the house, playing with members of the family or his toys.

The field dog that is regularly worked usually gets enough exercise, at least during the hunting season. For the dog that is not worked under the gun, trotting alongside a bicycle or chasing and returning a thrown object will help to keep him in trim flesh.

The authors feel that most Pointers are healthier in country or rural areas where they can exercise more vigorously. The Pointer in the country has much more freedom and should be let out for his exercise. If you plan to build a run, make it as large as possible and allow your pet outside the run at least once a day for an hour or so in order to stretch his legs and keep up his tone. An occasional session in the woods and fields will keep him exercised and alert. Many dogs also enjoy a swim during the summer—you can take your dog along to the old swimming hole for a cool swim. He'll also enjoy pursuing a ball in the water or a chase with an old friend.

If you have a puppy you may want playthings to distract him from your shoes or chairs. Most pet stores carry a supply of toys which are safe for dogs. Just be careful with rubber toys that your energetic puppy does not tear them apart and eat the pieces. Toys are not on his diet list! The safest toys are the natural rawhide "bones" offered at most pet stores. Nylon "bones" with natural scents are also available. Even a discarded rag doll or a knotted towel can provide amusement for a dog.

If you use your dog for hunting, it is wise to get him in shape before the hunting season by runs in the fields and woods. Increase the exercise gradually until he is conditioned for the long hours in the field.

If you give your dog adequate exercise together with proper grooming, diet and medical care, he will reward you with compliments from the neighbors, perhaps a blue ribbon at the dog show, or a bagful of game!

Chapter XII

Diseases and First Aid

The dog is heir to many illnesses, and, as with man, it seems that when one dread form has been overcome by some specific medical cure, another quite as lethal takes its place. It is held by some that this cycle will always continue, since it is Nature's basic way of controlling population.

There are, of course, several ways to circumvent Dame Nature's lethal plans. The initial step in this direction is to put the health of your dog in the hands of one who has the knowledge and equipment to cope competently with canine health problems. We mean, of course, a modern veterinarian. Behind this man are years of study and experience and a knowledge of all the vast research, past and present, which has developed the remarkable cures and artificial immunities that have so drastically lowered the canine mortality rate.

Put your trust in the qualified veterinarian and "beware of Greeks bearing gifts." Beware, too, of helpful friends who say, "I know what the trouble is and how to cure it. The same thing happened to my dog." Home doctoring by unskilled individuals acting upon the advice of unqualified "experts" has killed more dogs than distemper.

Your puppy is constantly exposed to innumerable diseases transmitted by flying and jumping insects, parasites, bacteria, fungus and virus. His body develops defenses and immunities against many of these diseases, but there are many more which we must cure (or immunize him against) if we want him to live his full span.

You are not qualified to treat your dog for many illnesses with the skill or knowledge necessary for success. This book can only give you a resume of modern findings on the most prevalent diseases and illnesses so that you can, in some instances, eliminate them or the causative agent by yourself. Even more important, this chapter will help you recognize disease symptoms in time to seek the aid of your veterinarian.

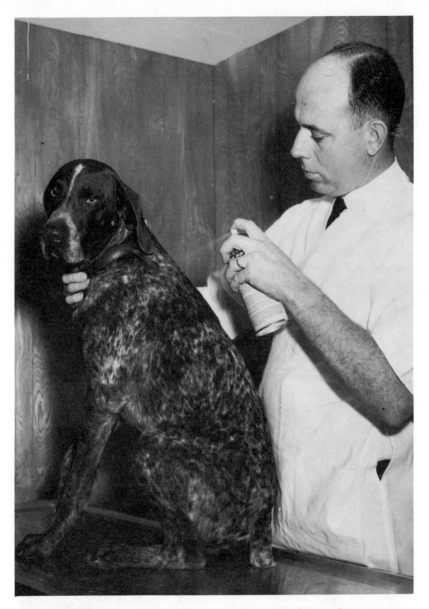

The modern small animal veterinarian is the graduate of a comprehensive course of study that is almost on a parallel with human medicine. Your veterinarian is the man to consult when any problems of health are presented, and a visit to him is definitely preferable than fooling with home remedies.

Many illnesses have an incubation period, during the early stages of which the animal himself may not show the symptoms of the disease, but can readily infect other dogs with which he comes in contact. It is readily seen, then, that places where many dogs are gathered together are particularly dangerous to your dog's health.

Parasitic diseases, which we will first consider, must not be taken too lightly, though they are the easiest of the diseases to cure. Great suffering and even death can come to your pup through these parasites if you neglect to realize the importance of both cure and the control of reinfestation.

EXTERNAL PARASITES

The lowly flea is one of the most dangerous insects from which you must protect your dog. It carries and spreads tapeworm, heartworm and bubonic plague, causes loss of coat and weight, spreads skin disease, and brings untold misery to its poor host. These pests

Where numbers of dogs are kept kenneled it is important to maintain constant hygiene so as to retard parasites. Prevention is the watchword here as there is much more work in getting rid of these pests as in keeping them out from the beginning.

are particularly difficult to combat because their eggs—of which they lay thousands—can lie dormant for months, hatching when conditions of moisture and warmth are present. Thus you may think you have rid your dog (and your house) of these devils, only to find that they mysteriously reappear as weather conditions change.

When your dog has fleas, use any good commercial flea powder which contains fresh rotenone. Dust him freely with the powder. It is not necessary to cover the dog completely, since the flea is active and will quickly reach a spot saturated with the powder and die. Rotenone is also fatal to lice. A solution of this drug in pine oil and added to water to be employed as a dip or rinse will kill all insects except ticks. DDT in liquid soap is excellent and long-potent, its effects lasting for as long as a week. Benzene hexachloride, chlordane, and any number of many new insecticides developed for the control of flies are also lethal to fleas. Whatever specific you use should also be used on your dog's sleeping quarters as well as on the animal itself. Repeat the treatment in ten days to eliminate fleas which have been newly hatched from dormant eggs.

TICKS

There are many kinds of ticks, all of which go through similar stages in their life process. At some stage in their lives they all find it necessary to feed on blood. Luckily, these insect vampires are fairly easily controlled. The female of the species is much larger than the male, which will generally be found hiding under the female. Care must be taken in the removal of these pests to guard against the mouth parts remaining embedded in the host's skin when the body of the tick is removed. DDT is an effective tick remover. Ether or nail-polish remover, touched to the individual tick, will cause it to relax its grip and fall off the host. The heated head of a match from which the flame has been just extinguished, employed in the same fashion, will cause individual ticks to release their hold and fall from the dog. After veterinary tick treatment, no attempt should be made to remove the pests manually, since the treatment will cause them to drop by themselves as they succumb.

MITES

There are three basic species of mites that generally infect dogs, the demodectic mange mite (red mange), the sarcoptic mange mite (white mange), and the ear mite. Demodectic mange is generally recognized by balding areas on the face, cheeks, and the front parts of the foreleg, which present a moth-eaten appearance. Reddening of the skin and great irritation occurs as a result of the frantic rubbing and scratching of affected parts by the animal. Rawness and thickening of the skin follows. Not too long ago this was a dread disease in dogs, from which few recovered. It is still a persistent and not easily cured condition unless promptly diagnosed and diligently attended to.

Sarcoptic mange mites can infest you as well as your dog. The resulting disease is known as scabies. This disease very much resembles dry dermatitis, or what is commonly called "dry eczema." The coat falls out and the denuded area becomes inflamed and itches constantly.

Ear mites, of course, infest the dog's ear and can be detected by an accumulation of crumbly dark brown or black wax within the ear. Shaking of the head and frequent scratching at the site of the infestation accompanied by squeals and grunting also is symptomatic of

Ear mites can become a chronic problem if they are allowed to go unchecked. Canker can result from an ear mite infection, causing tremendous discomfort to the affected dog. Your veterinarian is in the best position to treat the problem.

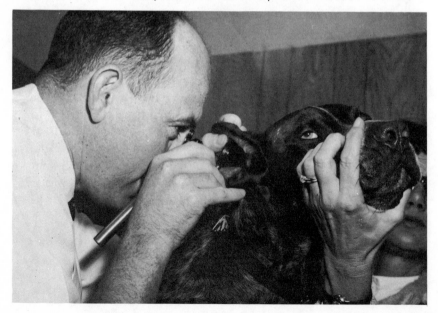

the presence of these pests. Canker of the ear is a condition, rather than a specific disease, which covers a wide range of ear infection and which displays symptoms similar to ear mite infection.

All three of these diseases and ear canker should be treated by your veterinarian. By taking skin scrapings or wax particles from the ear for microscopic examination, he can make an exact diagnosis and recommend specific treatment. The irritations caused by these ailments, unless immediately controlled, can result in loss of appetite and weight, and so lower your dog's natural resistance that he is open to the attack of other diseases which his bodily defenses could normally battle successfully.

1. Flea-host tapeworm, 2. Segment of tapeworm as seen in a dog's stool, 3. Common roundworm, 4. Whipworm, 5. Hookworm, 6. Heartworm.

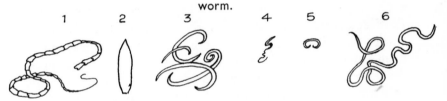

INTERNAL PARASITES

It seems strange, in the light of new discovery of specific controls for parasitism, that the incidence of parasitic infestation should still be almost as great as it was years ago. This can only be due to lack of realization by the dog owner of the importance of initial prevention and control against reinfestation. Strict hygiene must be adhered to if pups are not to be immediately reinfested. This is particularly true where worms are concerned.

In attempting to rid our dogs of worms, we must not be swayed by amateur opinion. The so-called "symptoms" of worms may be due to many other reasons. We may see the actual culprits in the animal's stool, but even then it is not wise to worm indiscriminately. The safest method to pursue is to take a small sample of your puppy's stool to your veterinarian. By a fecal analysis he can advise just what specific types of worms infest your dog and what drugs should be used to eliminate them.

Do not worm your puppy because you "think" he should be

wormed, or because you are advised to do so by some self-confessed "authority." Drugs employed to expel worms can prove highly dangerous to your pup if used indiscriminately and carelessly, and in many instances the same symptoms that are indicative of the presence of internal parasites can also be the signs of some other affliction.

A word here in regard to that belief that garlic will "cure" worms. Garlic is an excellent flavoring agent, favored by gourmets the world over—but—it will not rid your dog of worms. Its only curative power lies in the fact that, should you use it on a housedog who has worms, the first time he pants in your face you will definitely be cured of ever attempting this pseudo-remedy again.

ROUNDWORM

These are the most common worms found in dogs and can have grave effects upon puppies, which they almost invariably infest. Potbellies, general unthriftiness, diarrhea, coughing, lack of appetite, anemia, are the symptoms. They can also cause verminous pneumonia when in the larval stage. Fecal examinations of puppy stools should be made by your veterinarian frequently if control of these parasites is to be constant. Although, theoretically, it is possible for small puppies to be naturally worm free, actually most pups are born infested or contract the parasitic eggs at the mother's teat.

The roundworm lives in the intestine and feeds on the pup's partially digested food, growing and laying eggs which are passed out in the pup's stool to be picked up by him in various ways and so cause reinfestation. The life history of all the intestinal worms is a vicious circle, with the dog the beginning and the end host. This worm is yellowish-white in color and is shaped like a common garden worm, pointed at both ends. It is usually curled when found in the stool. There are several different species of this type of worm. Some varieties are more dangerous than others. They discharge toxin within the pup, and the movement of larvae to important internal sections of the pup's body can cause death.

The two drugs most used by kennel owners for the elimination of roundworms are N-butyl-chloride and tetrachloroethylene, but there are a host of other drugs, new and old, that can also do the job efficiently. With most of the worm drugs, give no food to the dog for twenty-four hours, or in the case of puppies, twenty hours, previous to the time he is given the medicine. It is absolutely essential that this starvation limit be adhered to, particularly if the drug used is tetra-chloroethylene, since the existence of the slightest amount of food in the stomach or intestine can cause death. One tenth c.c. to each pound of the animal's weight is the dosage for tetrachloroethylene, followed in one hour with a milk-of-magnesia physic, *never* an oily physic. Food may be given two hours later.

N-butyl-chloride is less toxic if the pup has eaten some food during the supposed starvation period. The dosage is one c.c. for every ten pounds of the weight of the dog. Any safe physic may be administered an hour later, and the pup fed within two hours afterward. Large doses of this drug can be given grown dogs without danger, and will kill whipworms as well as roundworms. A second treatment should follow in two weeks. The effect of N-butyl-chloride is cumulative; therefore, when a large dosage is necessary, the total amount to be given can be divided into many small doses administered, one small dose at a time, over a period of hours. The object of this procedure is to prevent the dog from vomiting up the drug, which generally occurs when a large dose is given all at once. This method of ad-ministering the drug has been found to be very effective.

HOOKWORMS

These tiny leeches who live on the blood of your dog, which they get from the intestinal walls, cause severe anemia, groaning, fits, diarrhea, loss of appetite and weight, rapid breathing, and swelling of the legs. The same treatment used to eradicate roundworms will also expel hookworms.

Good food is essential for quick recovery, with added amounts of liver and raw meat incorporated in the diet. Blood transfusions are often necessary if the infestation has been heavy. If one infestation follows another, a certain degree of immunity to the effects of the parasite seems to be built up by the dog. A second treatment should be given two weeks following the initial treatment.

WHIPWORMS

These small, thin whiplike worms are found in the intestines and the caecum. Those found in the intestines are reached and killed by the same drugs used in the eradication of roundworms and hook-worms. Most worm medicines will kill these helminths if they reach them, but those which live in the caecum are very difficult to reach.

They exude toxins which cause debilitation, anemia, and allied ills, and are probably a contributing factor in lowering the resistance to the onslaught of other infections. The usual symptoms of worm infestation are present.

N-butyl-chloride, in dosage three times greater than the round-worm dosage, appears to be quite effective in reaching the caecum and ridding the grown dog of most of these pests. The drug is to be given following the twenty-four hour period of fasting. Administration of an anti-emetic is generally indicated to keep the dog from disgorging the drug.

Hydrogen peroxide administered as an enema is highly effective but very dangerous, and should be applied only by expert hands.

TAPEWORMS

Tapeworms are not easily diagnosed by fecal test, but are easily identified when visible in the dog's stool. The worm is composed

Internal parasites are not something the pet owner should tamper with. The veterinarian should make a microscopic analysis of the stool and administer the necessary medication based on his findings.

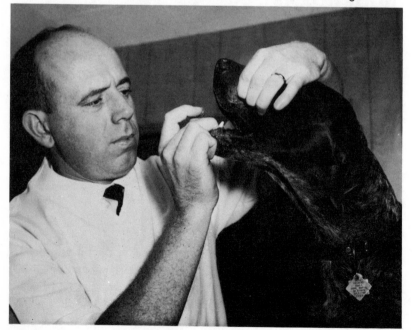

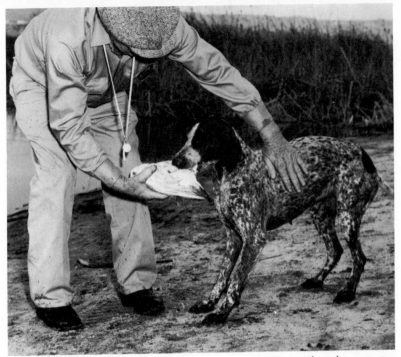

Those who use their dogs for hunting should constantly take care to see that their dogs do not become hosts to either internal or external parasites. There are many opportunities for these creatures to become established on a given dog and the owner's vigilance is required to keep an animal free of them.

of two distinct parts, the head and the segmented body. It is pieces of the segmented body that we see in the stools of the dog. They are usually pink or white, and flat. The common tapeworm, which is most prevalent in our dogs, is about eighteen inches long, and the larvae are carried by the flea. The head of the worm is smaller than a pinhead and attaches itself to the intestinal wall. Contrary to general belief, the puppy infested with tapeworms does not possess an enormous appetite—rather it fluctuates from good to poor. The animal shows the general signs of worm infestation. Often he squats and drags his hindquarters on the ground. This is due to tapeworm larvae moving and wriggling in the lower bowels. One must be careful in diagnosing this symptom, as it may also mean that the dog is suffering from distended anal glands.

Arecolene is an efficient expeller of tapeworms. Dosage is approximately one-tenth grain for every fifteen pounds of the dog's weight, administered after twenty hours of fasting. Nemural is also widely used. One pill for every eight pounds of body weight is given in a small amount of food after twelve hours of starvation. No worm medicine can be considered 100 percent effective in all cases. If one drug does not expel the worms satisfactorily, then another must be tried.

HEARTWORM

This villain inhabits the heart and is the most difficult to treat. The worm is about a foot long and literally stuffs the heart of the affected animal. It is prevalent in the southern states and has long been the curse of sporting-dog breeds. The worm is transmitted principally through the bite of an infected mosquito, which can fly from an infected southern canine visitor directly to your dog and do its dire deed.

The symptoms are: fatigue, gasping, coughing, nervousness, and sometimes dropsy and swelling of the extremities. Treatment for heartworms definitely must be left in the hands of your veterinarian. A wide variety of drugs are used in treatment. The most commonly employed are the arsenicals, antimony compounds, and caracide. Danger exists during cure when dying adult worms move to the lungs, causing suffocation, or when dead microfilariae, in a heavily infested dog, block the small blood vessels in the heart muscles. The invading microfilariae are not discernible in the blood until nine months following introduction of the disease by the bite of the carrier mosquito.

In an article on this subject in *Field and Stream* magazine, Joe Stetson describes a controlled experiment in which caracide was employed in periodic treatments as a preventive of heartworm. The experiment was carried out over a period of eighteen months, during which time the untreated dogs became positive for heartworm and eventually died. A post mortem proved the presence of the worm. The dogs that underwent scheduled prophylaxis have been found, by blood test, to be free of circulating microfilariae and are thriving.

COCCIDIOSIS

This disease is caused by a single-celled protozoa. It affects dogs of all ages, but is not dangerous to mature animals. When puppies become infected by a severe case of coccidiosis, it very often proves fatal, since it produces such general weakness and emaciation that the puppy has no defense against other invading harmful organisms. Loose and bloody stools are indicative of the presence of this disease, as is loss of appetite, weakness, emaciation, discharge from the eyes, and a fever of approximately 103 degrees. The disease is contracted directly or through flies that have come from infected quarters. Infection seems to occur over and over again, limiting the puppy's chance of recovery with each succeeding infection. The duration of the disease is about three weeks, but new infestations can stretch this period of illness on until your puppy has little chance to recover. Strict sanitation and supportive treatment of good nutrition— utilizing milk, fat, kaopectate, and bone ash with added dextrose and calcium—seem to be all that can be done in the way of treatment. Force feed the puppy if necessary. The more food that you can get into him to give him strength until the disease has run its course, the better will be his chances of recovery. Specific cures have been developed in other animals and poultry, but not as yet in dogs. Recovered dogs are life-long carriers of the disease.

SKIN DISEASES

Diseases of the skin in dogs are many, varied, and easily confused by the puppy owner. All skin afflictions should be immediately diagnosed and treated by your veterinarian. Whatever drug is prescribed must be employed diligently, and in quantity, and generally long after surface indications of the disease have ceased to exist. A surface cure may be attained, but the infection remains buried deep in the hair follicles or skin glands, to erupt again if treatment is suspended too soon. Contrary to popular belief, diet, if well balanced and complete, is seldom the cause of skin disease.

Eczema

The word "eczema" is a much-abused word, as is the word "dermatitis." Both are used with extravagance in the identification of various forms of skin disorders. We will concern ourselves with the two most prevalent forms of so-called eczema, namely wet eczema and dry eczema. In the wet form, the skin exudes moisture and then scabs over, due to constant scratching and biting by the dog at the site of infection. The dry form manifests itself in dry patches which irritate and itch, causing great discomfort to the dog. In both instances the hair falls out and the spread of the disease is rapid. The cause of these diseases is not yet known, though many are thought to be originated by various fungi and aggravated by allergic conditions. The quickest means of bringing these diseases under control is through the application of a good skin remedy often combined with a fungicide, which your veterinarian will prescribe. An over-all dip, employing specific liquid medication, is beneficial in many cases and has a continuing curative effect over a period of days.

Ringworm

This infection is caused by a fungus and is highly contagious to humans. In the dog it generally appears on the face as a round or oval spot from which the hair has fallen. Ringworm is easily cured by the application of iodine and glycerine (50 per cent of each ingredient) or a fungicide liberally applied. The new antibiotic Malucidin eliminates ringworm quickly and effectively.

Acne

Your puppy will frequently display small eruptions on the soft skin of his belly. These little pimples rupture and form a scab. The rash is caused by inflammation of the skin glands and is not a serious condition. Treatment consists of washing the affected area with alcohol or witch hazel, followed by the application of a healing lotion or powder, such as B.F.I., or Army Formula Foot Powder, which is similar to Quinsana.

Hookworm Larvae Infection

The skin of your pup can become infected from the eggs and larvae of the hookworm acquired from a muddy hookworm-infested run. The larvae becomes stuck to his coat with mud and burrow into the skin, leaving ugly raw red patches. One or two baths in warm water to which an antiseptic has been added usually cures the condition quickly.

DEFICIENCY DISEASES

These diseases, or conditions, are caused by dietary deficiencies or some condition which robs the diet of necessary ingredients. Anemia, a deficiency condition, is a shortage of hemoglobin. Hookworms, lice, and any disease that depletes the system of red blood cells, are contributory causes. A shortage or lack of specific minerals or vitamins in the diet can also cause anemia. Not so long ago, rickets was the most common of the deficiency diseases, caused by a lack of one or more of the dietary elements—vitamin D, calcium, and phosphorus. There are other types of deficiency diseases originating in dietary inadequacy and characterized by unthriftiness in one or more phases. The cure exists in supplying the missing food factors to the diet. Sometimes, even though all the necessary dietary elements are present in the food, some are destroyed by improper feeding procedure. For example, a substance in raw eggs, avertin, destroys biotin, one of the B-complex group of vitamins. Cooking will destroy the avertin in the egg white and prevent a biotin deficiency in the diet.

BACTERIAL DISEASES

In this group we find leptospirosis, tetanus, pneumonia, strep infections and many other dangerous diseases. The mortality rate is generally high in all of the bacterial diseases, and treatment should be left to your veterinarian.

Leptospirosis

Leptospirosis is spread most frequently by the urine of infected dogs, which can infect for six months or more after the animal has recovered from the disease. Rats are the carriers of the bacterial agent which produces this disease. A puppy will find a bone upon which an infected rat has urinated, chew the bone, and become infested with the disease in turn. Leptospirosis is primarily dangerous in the damage it does to the kidneys. Complete isolation of affected individuals to keep the disease from spreading and rat control are the chief means of prevention. Also, newly developed vaccines may be employed by your veterinarian as a preventive measure. Initial diagnosis is difficult, and the disease has generally made drastic inroads before a cure is effected. It has been estimated that fully 50 percent of all dogs throughout the world have been stricken with leptospirosis at one time or another and that in many instances the disease was not recognized for what it was. The disease produced by *Leptospira* in the blood of humans is known as Weil's disease.

Tetanus

Lockjaw bacteria produce an exceedingly deadly poison. The germs grow in the depths of a sealed-over wound where oxygen cannot penetrate. To prevent this disease, every deep wound acquired by your dog should be thoroughly cleansed and disinfected, and an antitoxin given the animal. Treatment follows the same general pattern as prevention. If the jaw locks, intravenous feeding must be given.

Strep throat

This is a very contagious disease caused by a specific group of bacteria labeled "streptococcus." Characteristic of this disease is the high temperature that accompanies infection (104 to 106 degrees). Other symptoms are loose stool at the beginning of the disease and a slight optic discharge. The throat becomes intensely inflamed, swallowing is difficult, and the glands under the ears are swollen. Immunity is developed by the host after the initial attack.

Tonsillitis

Inflammation of the tonsils can be either of bacterial or virus origin. It is not a serious disease in itself, but is often a symptom of other diseases. Tonsillitis is not to be confused with strep throat, which is produced by an entirely different organism. The symptoms of tonsillitis are enlarged and reddened tonsils, poor appetite, vomiting, and optic discharge. The disease usually runs its course in from five to seven days. Penicillin, aureomycin, terramycin, chloromycetin, etc., have been used with success in treatment.

Pneumonia

Pneumonia is a bacterial disease of the lungs of which the symptoms are poor appetite, optic discharge, shallow and rapid respiration. Affected animals become immune to the particular type of pneumonia from which they have recovered. Oral treatment utilizing antibiotic or sulfa drugs, combined with a pneumonia jacket of cloth or cotton padding wrapped around the chest area, seems to be standard treatment.

VIRAL DISEASES

The dread viral diseases are caused by the smallest organisms known to man. They live in the cells and often attack the nerve tissue. The tissue thus weakened is easily invaded by many types of bacteria. Complications then set in, and it is these accompanying ills which usually prove fatal. The secondary infections can be treated with several of the "wonder" drugs, and excellent care and nursing is necessary if the stricken animal is to survive. Your veterinarian is the only person qualified to aid your pup when a viral disease strikes.

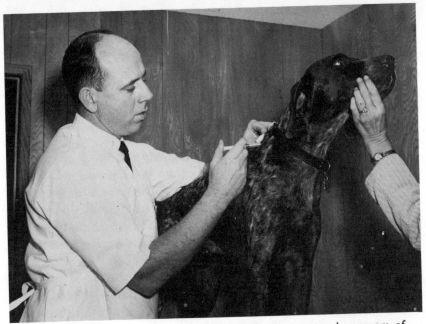

The cornerstone of canine preventive medicine is a sound program of protective inoculations against the major canine diseases. Recent study has disclosed that no inoculation is truly permanent and all dogs should receive an annual booster shot.

The diseases in this category include distemper, infectious hepatitis, rabies, kennel cough, housedog disease, and primary encephalitis—the latter actually inflammation of the brain, a condition characterizing several illnesses, particularly those of viral origin.

Distemper

Until recently a great many separate diseases had been lumped under the general heading of distemper. In the last few years modern science has isolated a number of separate diseases of the distemper complex, such as infectious hepatitis, hard-pad disease, influenza, and primary encephalitis, which had been diagnosed as distemper. Thus, with more accurate diagnosis, great strides have been made in conquering, not only distemper, but these other, allied diseases. Distemper (Carre) is now rare, due to successful methods of immunization, but any signs of illness in an animal not immunized may be the beginning of the disease. The symptoms are so similar to those of various other diseases that only a trained observer can diagnose correctly. Treatment consists of the use of drugs to counteract complications arising from the invasion of secondary diseases and in keeping the stricken animal warm, well fed, comfortable and free from dehydration until the disease has run its course. In many instances, even if the pup gets well, he will be left with some dreadful souvenir of the disease which will mar him for life. After-effects are common in most of the diseases of the distemper complex.

The tremendous value of immunization against this viral disease cannot be exaggerated. Except for the natural resistance your animal carries against disease, it is the one means of protection you have against this killer. There have been various methods of immunization developed in the last several years, but it would seem that the most recently favored is the avianized vaccine (or chick embryo-adapted vaccine). There are reasonably sure indications that this avianized vaccine protects against hard-pad disease and primary encephalitis as well as distemper. Injections can be given at any age, even as early as six or eight weeks, with a repeat dosage at six months of age. It does not affect the tissues, nor can it cause any ill effects to other dogs who come in contact with the vaccinated animal.

Infectious hepatitis

This disease attacks dogs of all ages, but is particularly deadly to puppies. We see young puppies in the nest, healthy, bright and sturdy; suddenly they begin to vomit, and the next day they are dead of infectious hepatitis—it strikes that quickly. The disease is almost impossible to diagnose correctly, and there is no known treatment that will cure it. Astute authorities claim that if an afflicted dog survives three days after the onslaught of the disease he will, in all probability, completely recover. Research is under way at present upon a vaccine that could afford safe and effective protection against infectious hepatitis.

Rabies

This is the most terrible of diseases, since it knows no bounds. It is transmissible to all kinds of animals and birds, including the superior animal, man. To contract this dread disease, the dog must be bitten by a rabid animal or the rabies virus must enter the body through a broken skin surface. The disease incubation period is governed by the distance of the virus point of entry to the brain. The closer the point of entry is to the brain, the quicker the disease manifests itself. We can be thankful that rabies is not nearly as prevalent as is supposed

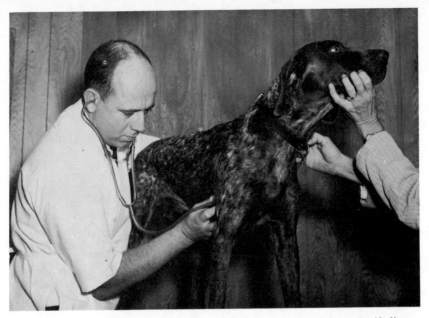

An annual check-up is as wise a plan for your dog as it is for you. If all is well with him you have peace of mind as to your dog's health, but if something needs attention your veterinarian can advise you and treat him at the same time.

by the uninformed. Restlessness, excitability, perverted appetite, character reversal, wildness, drowsiness, loss of acuteness of senses, (and of feeling, in some instances) foaming at the mouth, and many other lesser symptoms come with the onslaught of this disease. Diagnosis by trained persons of a portion of the brain is conceded to be the only way of determining whether an animal died of rabies or of one of the distemper complex diseases. Very little has been done in introducing drugs or specifics that can give satisfaction in combating this disease; perhaps evaluation of the efficacy of such products is almost impossible with a disease so rare and difficult to diagnose.

In 1948 an avianized, modified live virus vaccine was reported, and is being used in clinical trials with some success. Quarantine, such as that pursued in England, even of six months' duration, is still not the answer to the rabies question, though it is undeniably effective. It is, however, not proof positive. Recently a dog on arriving in England was held in quarantine for the usual six months. The day before he was to be released to his owners, the attendant noticed that he was acting strangely. He died the next day. Under examination his brain showed typical inclusion bodies, establishing the fact that he had died of rabies. This is a truly dangerous disease that can bring frightful death to animal or man. When an effective way of immunization is found and recommended by authoritative sources, it should be the duty of every dog owner to protect his dog, himself, his family, and neighbors from even the slight risk that exists of contracting rabies by taking immediate advantage in this form of protection.

FITS

Fits in dogs are symptoms of diseases rather than illness itself. They can be caused by the onslaught of any number of diseases, including worms, distemper, epilepsy, primary encephalitis, poisoning, etc. Running fits can also be traced to dietary deficiencies. The underlying reason for the fits, or convulsions, must be diagnosed by your veterinarian and the cause treated.

DIARRHEA

Diarrhea, which is officially defined as watery movements occurring eight or more times a day, is often a symptom of one of many other diseases. But, if on taking your dog's temperature, you find there is no fever, it is quite possible the condition has been caused by either a change of diet, of climate or water, or even by a simple intestinal disturbance. A tightening agent such as Kaopectate should be given. Water should be withheld and corn syrup, dissolved in boiled milk, substituted to prevent dehydration in the patient. Feed hard-boiled eggs, boiled milk, meat, cheese, boiled white rice, cracker, kibbles, or dog biscuits. Add a tablespoonful of bone ash (not bone meal) to the diet. If the condition is not corrected within two or three days, if there is an excess of blood passed in the stool, or if signs of other illness become manifest, don't delay a trip to your veterinarian.

CONSTIPATION

If the dog's stool is so hard that it is difficult for him to pass it and he strains and grunts during the process, then he is obviously constipated. The cause of constipation is diet. Bones and dog biscuits, given abundantly, can cause this condition, as can any of the items

The above illustration shows a good way to have to get to the veterinarian in a large hurry. Pulling on a puppy's front legs in this fashion can result in a serious sprain and quite possibly, can affect the youngster's front end for life.

of diet mentioned above as treatment for diarrhea. Chronic constipation can result in hemorrhoids which, if persistent, must be removed by surgery. The cure for constipation and its accompanying ills is the introduction of laxative food elements into the diet. Stewed tomatoes, buttermilk, skim milk, whey, bran, alfalfa meal, and various fruits can be fed and a bland physic given. Enemas can bring quick relief. Once the condition is rectified, the dog should be given a good balanced diet, avoiding all types of foods that will produce constipation.

EYE AILMENTS

The eyes are not only the mirror of the soul, they are also the mirror of many kinds of disease. Discharge from the eyes is one of the many symptoms warning of most internal viral, parasitic, and bacterial diseases. Of the ailments affecting the eye itself, the most usual are: glaucoma, which seems to be a hereditary disease; pink eye, a strep infection; cataracts; opacity of the lens in older dogs; corneal opacity, such as follows some cases of infectious hepatitis; and teratoma. Mange, fungus, inturned lids, and growths on the lid are other eye ailments. The wise procedure is to consult your veterinarian for specific treatment.

When the eyes show a discharge from reasons other than those that can be labeled "ailment", such as irritation from dust, wind, or sand, they should be washed with warm water on cotton or a soft cloth. After gently washing the eyes, an ophthalmic ointment combining a mild anesthetic and antiseptic can be utilized. Butyl sulphate, 1 percent yellow oxide of mercury, and 5 percent sulphathiazole ointment are all good. Boric acid seems to be falling out of favor as an opthalmic antiseptic. The liquid discharged by the dog's tear ducts is a better antiseptic, and much cheaper.

ANAL GLANDS

If your male dog consistently drags his rear parts on the ground or bites this area, the cause is probably impacted anal glands. These glands, which are located on each side of the anus, should be periodically cleared by squeezing. The job is not a nice one, and can be much more effectively done by your veterinarian. Unless these glands are kept reasonably clean, infection can become housed in this site, resulting in the formation of an abscess which will need surgical care.

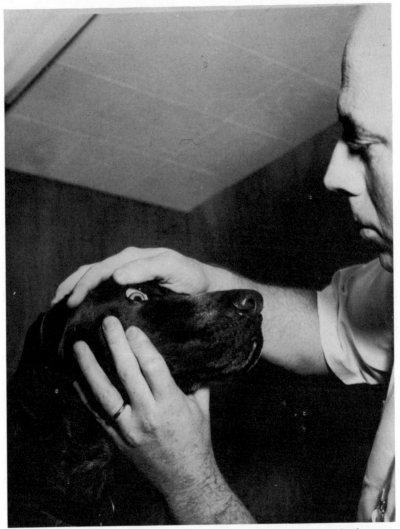

There is much that a veterinarian can tell from looking into a dog's eyes. Any dullness, unusual discharge or general change in appearance can be a sign of approaching trouble and should be called to the attention of your veterinarian at once.

Dogs that get an abundance of exercise seldom need the anal glands attended to.

The many other ailments which your dog is heir to, such as cancer, tumors, rupture, heart disease, fractures, and the results of accidents, must all be diagnosed and tended to by your veterinarian. When you go to your veterinarian with a sick dog, always remember to bring along a sample of his stool for analysis. Many times samples of his urine are needed, too. Your veterinarian is the only one qualified to treat your dog for disease, but protection against disease is to a great extent in the hands of the dog owner. If those hands are capable, a great deal of pain and misery for both dog and owner can be eliminated. Death can be cheated, investment saved, and veterinary bills kept to a minimum. A periodic health check by your veterinarian is a wise investment.

ADMINISTERING MEDICATION

Some people seem to have ten thumbs on each hand when they attempt to give medicine to their dog. They become agitated and approach the task with so little sureness that their mood is communicated to the patient, increasing the difficulties. Invite calmness and quietness in the patient by emanating these qualities yourself. Speak to the animal in low, easy tones, petting him slowly, quieting him down in preparation. The administration of medicine should be made without fuss and as though it is some quiet and private new game between you and your dog.

At the corner of your dog's mouth there is a lip pocket perfect for the administering of liquid medicine if used correctly. Have the animal sit, then raise his muzzle so that his head is slanted upward looking toward the sky. Slide two fingers in the corner of his mouth where the upper and lower lip edges join, pull gently outward, and you have a pocket between the cheek flesh and the gums. Into this pocket pour the liquid medicine slowly. Keep his head up, and the liquid will run from the pocket into his throat and he will swallow it. Continue this procedure until the complete dose has been given. This will be easier to accomplish if the medicine has been spooned into a small bottle. The bottle neck, inserted into the lip pocket, is tipped, and the contents will slowly run down his throat.

To give pills or capsules, the head of the patient must again be raised with muzzle pointing upward. With one hand, grasp the cheeks of the pup just behind the lip edges where the teeth come

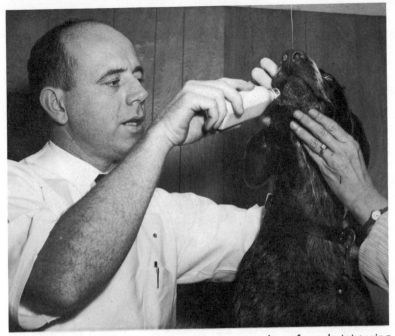

If you are unfamiliar with the proper procedure for administering medications to your dog your veterinarian will be happy to show you exactly how it should be done for solids as well as for liquids.

together on the inside of the mouth. With the thumb on one side and the fingers on the other, press inward as though squeezing. The lips are pushed against the teeth, and the pressure of your fingers forces the mouth open. The dog will not completely close his mouth, since doing so would cause him to bite his lips. With your other hand, insert the pill in the patient's mouth as far back on the base of the tongue as you can, pushing it back with your second finger. Withdraw your hand quickly, allow the dog to close his mouth, and hold it closed with your hand, but not too tightly. Massage the dog's throat and watch for the tip of his tongue to show between his front teeth, signifying the fact that the capsule or pill has been swallowed.

In taking your dog's temperature, an ordinary rectal thermometer is adequate. It must be first shaken down, then dipped in vaseline, and inserted into the rectum for approximately three-quarters of its length. Allow it to remain there for no less than a full minute, restraining the dog from sitting during that time. When withdrawn, it should be wiped with a piece of cotton, read, then washed in alcohol—never hot water. The arrow on most thermometers at 98.6 degrees indicates normal human temperature and should be disregarded. Normal temperature for your grown dog is 101 degrees; normal dog temperature varies between $101\frac{1}{2}$ and 102 degrees. Excitement can raise the temperature, so it is best to take a reading only when the dog is calm.

In applying an ophthalmic ointment to the eye, simply pull the lower lid out, squeeze a small amount of ointment into the pocket thus produced, and release the lid. The dog will blink, and the ointment will spread over the eye.

Should you find it necessary to give your dog an enema, employ an ordinary human-size bag and rubber hose. Simply grease the catheter with vaseline and insert the hose well into the rectum. The bag should be held high for a constant flow of water. A quart of warm soapy water or plain water with a tablespoonful of salt makes an efficient enema for a big dog. Puppies need proportionately less.

FIRST AID

Emergencies quite frequently occur which make it necessary for you to care for the dog yourself until veterinary aid is available. Quite often emergency help by the owner can save the pup's life or lessen the chance of permanent injury. A badly injured animal, blinded to all else but abysmal pain, often reverts to the primitive, wanting only to be left alone with his misery. Injured, panic-stricken, not recognizing you, he might attempt to bite when you wish to help him. Under the stress of fright and pain, this reaction is normal in animals. A muzzle can easily be slipped over his foreface, or a piece of bandage or strip of cloth can be fashioned into a muzzle by looping it around the dog's muzzle, crossing it under the jaws, and bringing the two ends around in back of the dog's head and tying them. Snap a leash onto his collar as quickly as possible to prevent him from running away and hiding. If it is necessary to lift him, grasp him by the neck, getting as large a handful of skin as you can, as high up on the neck as possible. Hold tight and he won't be able to turn his head far enough around to bite. Lift him off the ground by the hold you have on his neck, encircle his body with your other arm, and support him or carry him.

Every dog owner should have handy a first-aid kit specifically for the use of his dog. It should contain a thermometer, surgical scissors, rolls of three-inch and six-inch bandage, a roll of one-inch adhesive tape, a package of surgical cotton, a jar of vaseline, enema equipment, bulb syringe, ten c.c. hypodermic syringe, flea powder, skin remedy, tweezers, ophthalmic ointment, paregoric, Kaopectate, peroxide of hydrogen, merthiolate, Army Formula Foot Powder, alcohol, ear remedy, aspirin, milk of magnesia, castor oil, mineral oil, and dressing salve.

Here are two charts for your reference, one covering general first-aid measures and the other a chart of poisons and antidotes. Remember that in most instances these are emergency measures, not specific treatments, and are designed to help you in aiding your pup until you can reach your veterinarian.

FIRST-AID CHART

Emergency	Treatment	Remarks
Accidents	Automobile, Treat for shock. If gums are white, indicates probable internal injury. Wrap bandage tightly around body until it forms a sheath. Keep very quiet until veterinarian comes.	Call veterinarian immediately.
Bee stings	Give paregoric or aspirin to ease pain. If in state of shock, treat for same.	Call veterinarian for advice.
Bites (animal)	Tooth wounds—area should be shaved and antiseptic solution flowed into punctures, with eye dropper. Iodine, merthiolate, etc., can be used. If badly bitten or ripped, take dog to your veterinarian for treatment.	If superficial wounds become infected after first aid, consult veterinarian.
Bloat	Stomach distends like a balloon. Pierce stomach wall with hollow needle to allow gas to escape. Follow with stimulant—2 cups of coffee. Then treat for shock.	
Burns	Apply strong, body heat strained tea to burned area, followed by covering of vaseline.	Unless burn is very minor, consult veterinarian immediately.
Broken bones	If break involves a limb, fashion splint to keep immobile. If ribs, pelvis, shoulder, or back involved, keep dog from moving until professional help comes.	Call veterinarian immediately.

Choking	If bone, wood, or any foreign object can be seen at back of mouth or throat remove with fingers. If object can't be removed or is too deeply imbedded or too far back in throat, rush to veterinarian immediately.	
Cuts	Minor cuts: allow dog to lick and cleanse. If not within his reach, clean cut with peroxide, then apply merthiolate. Severe cuts: apply pressure bandage to stop bleeding—a wad of bandage over wound and bandage wrapped tightly over it. Take to veterinarian.	If cut becomes infected or needs suturing, consult veterinarian.
Dislocations	Keep dog quiet and take to veterinarian at once.	
Drowning	Artificial respiration. Lay dog on his side, push with hand on his ribs, release quickly. Repeat every 2 seconds. Treat for shock.	New method of artificial respiration as employed by fire department useful here.
Electric shock	Artificial respiration. Treat for shock.	Call veterinarian immediately.
Heat stroke	Quickly immerse the dog in cold water until relief is given. Give cold water enema. Or lay dog flat and pour cold water over him, turn electric fan on him, and continue pouring cold water as it evaporates.	Cold towel pressed against abdomen aids in reducing temp. quickly if quantity of water not available.
Porcupine quills	Tie dog up, hold him between knees, and pull all quills out with pliers. Don't forget tongue and inside of mouth.	See veterinarian to remove quills too deeply imbedded.
Shock	Cover dog with blanket. Administer stimulant (coffee with sugar). Allow him to rest, and soothe with voice and hand.	Alcoholic beverages are NOT stimulants.
Snake bite	Cut deep X over fang marks. Drop potassium-permanganate into cut. Apply tourniquet above bite if on foot or leg.	Apply first aid only if a veterinarian or a doctor can't be reached.

POISON	HOUSEHOLD ANTIDOTE
ACIDS	Bicarbonate of soda
ALKALIES	Vinegar or lemon juice
(cleansing agents)	
ARSENIC	Epsom salts
HYDROCYANIC ACID	Dextrose or corn sirup
(wild cherry; laurel leaves)	
LEAD	Epsom salts
(paint pigments)	
PHOSPHORUS	Peroxide of hydrogen
(rat poison)	
MERCURY	Eggs and milk
THEOBROMINE	Phenobarbital
(cooking chocolate)	
THALLIUM	Table salt in water
(bug poisons)	
FOOD POISONING	Peroxide of hydrogen, followed by enema
(garbage, etc.)	
STRYCHNINE	Sedatives. Phenobarbital, Nembutal.
DDT	Peroxide and enema

INDEX